International Perspectives on Early Years Workforce Development

CRITICAL APPROACHES TO THE EARLY YEARS

You might also like the following books from Critical Publishing

Developing as a Reflective Early Years Professional: A Thematic Approach
Carol Hayes et al
978-1-909682-21-4 Published June 2014

Early Years Policy and Practice: A Critical Alliance
Pat Tomlinson
978-1-909330-61-0 Published September 2013

Teaching and Learning Early Years Mathematics: Subject and Pedagogic Knowledge
Mary Briggs
978-1-909330-37-5 Published September 2013

Teaching Systematic Synthetic Phonics and Early English
Jonathan Glazzard and Jane Stokoe
978-1-909330-09-2 Published March 2013

The Critical Years: Early Years Development from Conception to 5
Tim Gully
978-1-909330-73-3 Published June 2014

Well-being in the Early Years
Ed Chelle Davison and Susan Waltham
978-1-909330-65-8 Published September 2013

Early Years Placements: A Critical Guide to Outstanding Work-based Learning
Jackie Musgrave and Nicola Stobbs
978-1-909682-65-8 March 2015

Most of our titles are also available in a range of electronic formats. To order please go to our website www.criticalpublishing.com or contact our distributor, NBN International, 10 Thornbury Road, Plymouth PL6 7PP, telephone 01752 202301 or email orders@nbninternational.com.

International Perspectives on Early Years Workforce Development

Edited by
Verity Campbell-Barr & Jan Georgeson
Series Editor Chelle Davison

CRITICAL
APPROACHES
TO THE EARLY
YEARS

British Library Cataloguing in Publication Data
A CIP record for this book is available from the British Library

ISBN: 978-1-909682-77-1

This book is also available in the following e-book formats:

MOBI: 978-1-909682-78-8
EPUB: 978-1-909682-79-5
Adobe e-book reader: 978-1-909682-80-1

Cover and text design by Greensplash Limited
Project Management by Out of House Publishing
Typeset by Newgen Knowledge Works
Printed and bound in Great Britain by Bell & Bain, Glasgow

Critical Publishing
152 Chester Road
Northwich
CW8 4AL
www.criticalpublishing.com

Contents

Meet the series editor and book editors

Chelle Davison is head of department, undergraduate ITE, in the Faculty of Education, Arts and Business at the University of Cumbria. The Department has over 450 trainees studying early years, primary, secondary and SEN initial teacher education. Chelle has made a significant contribution to a range of policy documents and government reviews, and is a devoted supporter of the professionalisation of the early years workforce.

Verity Campbell-Barr is a lecturer in early childhood studies at the Plymouth Institute of Education, Plymouth University. Her research interests include the mixed economy of childcare and early years education provision, experiences of working in early childhood occupations, the role of childcare in supporting employment and the welfare to work agenda, and understanding quality childcare and early years education from multiple perspectives.

Jan Georgeson is a research fellow in early education development at the Plymouth Institute of Education, Plymouth University. Her role involves developing and conducting independent research projects and collaborating with colleagues in the development of research within the School of Education, and she has a particular interest in research methods. She is currently researching the professionalisation of the early years workforce and early cognitive development, including the role of parents, practitioners and other caregivers.

About the contributors

Lynn Blakemore is a lecturer for childhood studies at the University Centre, Highlands College in Jersey and is currently engaged in research exploring the development of computing and computational skills in the primary curriculum.

Ingegerd Tallberg Broman is professor of education with a focus on younger children in the Children, Youth and Society department at Malmö University, and is responsible for the research environment and the national graduate school of the same name.

Federica Caruso is currently a research assistant at the Institute of Education at Plymouth University while completing her PhD on multi-professional practices in children's centres.

Claire Farley is a visiting lecturer for childhood studies at the University Centre, Highlands College in Jersey, and is presently engaged in research with young people exploring the right to vote at 16 in Jersey.

Noirin Hayes is visiting professor developing early education research at the School of Education, Trinity College, Dublin, and has particular interests in quality early years pedagogy and early years policy.

Ulrike Hohmann is a senior lecturer in the Institute of Education at Plymouth University and teaches on a variety of undergraduate and postgraduate programmes in early childhood studies.

Balázs Molnár is a senior lecturer in the Faculty of Child and Adult Education at the University of Debrecen, Hungary, and teaches research methodology and play-based learning in the kindergarten.

Colette Murphy is director of research at Trinity College, Dublin, where she also teaches socio-cultural issues in science education and research with children on postgraduate courses.

Sándor Pálfi is professor and head of the Department of Child Education at the University of Debrecen in Hungary and teaches basic principles of kindergarten pedagogy, alternative pedagogy and play-based education.

Greg Tabios Pawilen is currently chief education specialist for the Division of Governance and Coordination of the Commission on Higher Education in the Philippines, and serves as curriculum consultant on early childhood education and teacher education projects.

Sven Persson is professor in pedagogy at the Faculty for Learning and Society, and Director of the Centre for Professional Studies at Malmö University, and researches and teaches on diversity, childhood and educational actions in preschool.

Frances Press is associate professor at Charles Stuart University, Bathurst, Australia, where she teaches and researches in early childhood education and has recently completed a history of early childhood in Australia.

Philip Selbie lectures in early childhood studies on BA, BEd and MA programmes at Plymouth University, with particular interests in young children's spirituality and the history and philosophy of early childhood education.

Paolo Sorzio is a lecturer in education at the University of Trieste, Italy. His research interests are in curriculum theory and teachers' professionalism.

Manabu Sumida is an associate professor of science education at the Faculty of Education, Ehime University, Japan. His research areas are culture studies in science education and science education for the early childhood years.

Sándor Szerepi is associate professor in the Department of Child Education, Faculty of Child and Adult Education at the University of Debrecen, Hungary, teaching pedagogy, social work and history.

Anikó Nagy Varga is a senior lecturer in the Department of Child Education at the University of Debrecen in Hungary, where she teaches basic principles of pedagogy, family pedagogy, understanding the world and associated methods.

Acknowledgements

We would like to thank our contributors for writing interesting, well-informed chapters that share their knowledge of issues for early years workforce development around the world, which turned out to be just what we were hoping for. We are also grateful for their patience and responsiveness to our requests for tweaks and changes.

The authors of Chapter 3 'Russia: Golden Key Schools' would like to acknowledge the work of Marie-Louise Murphy, one of the team of internationals who visited Golden Key Schools in Belaya Kalitva and Moscow, in the preparation of their chapter.

The author of Chapter 6 'The Australian ECEC workforce: feminism, feminisation and fragmentation' would like to thank her friend and colleague Dr Sandie Wong for her unfailing efforts to uncover the gems of early childhood history.

We are also grateful to Julia Morris at Critical Publishing for her patience as the book emerged from our original idea through perhaps a more organic process than she might have liked, and for having faith that it would indeed mature to fruition at more or less the time we said it would.

Finally, we would like to thank Matt and Mark for their unquestioning support, tolerance of curtailed weekends and timely supply of tea and coffee.

Preface: introduction to critical thinking

What is critical thinking?

This section gives you the opportunity to learn more about critical thinking and the skills you will acquire as you use this series. It will introduce you to the meaning of critical thinking and how you can develop the necessary skills to read and research effectively towards a critical approach to learning and analysis. It is a necessary and wholly beneficial position to be starting with questions and finishing your journey with more questions.

> *Judge a man by his questions rather than by his answers*
> (François-Marie Arouet (Voltaire))

If you are already a professional within the early years sector, maybe as a teacher in a reception class, or as an early years educator in a private daycare setting, you will no doubt have faced many challenging debates, discussions at training events and your own personal questioning of the policies faced by the sector as a whole. We want you to ask these questions. More importantly we believe it to be an essential and crucial part of your professional development. You will no doubt be required to implement the policies that might at first seem so detached from your day-to-day teaching and practice. It is critical that you question these policies, that you understand their purpose, and moreover that you understand how they have come to being.

Often students are faced with complex definitions of critical thinking that require them to deconstruct the concept before they fully understand just how to *do* critical thinking in the first place. For example,

> *Critical thinking is the intellectually disciplined process of actively and skilfully conceptualizing, applying, analysing, synthesizing, and/or evaluating information gathered from, or generated by, observation, experience, reflection, reasoning, or communication, as a guide to belief and action.*
> (Scriven and Paul, 1989)

Rather than confusing you with academic definitions, it is our hope that as you read further and begin to understand this topic more, you will be encouraged to ask contemplative questions. Alison King emphasises the importance of students acquiring and cultivating *'a habit of inquiry'* (1995, p 13) to enable them to *'learn to ask thoughtful questions'* (King, 1995). Contrary to the standard methods of 'instruction' that leaves students as passive recipients of information, King argues that where students have developed the skills of critical thinking they become 'autonomous' learners:

> *Such a habit of inquiry learned and practised in class can be applied also to their everyday lives: to what they see on television, read in the newspaper, observe in popular culture and hear during interaction with friends and colleagues, as well as to decisions they make about personal relationships, consumer purchases, political choices, and business transactions.*

> (King, 1995, p 13)

Consider the subject matter that you are now researching; you may have been tasked with the question 'How has policy changed over the past 25 years?' This is what King would suggest is a 'factual' question, one that may well have a limited answer. Once you have this answer, there is a tendency to stop there, making the inquiry fact-based rather than critical. If you were to follow this first question up with a critical question, King would argue that you are beginning to *'introduce high level cognitive processes such as analysis of ideas, comparison and contrast, inference, prediction [and] evaluation'* (1995, p 140).

Example:

Factual question	Critical question
How has policy changed over the past 25 years?	What has been the impact of policy change over the past 25 years?
Which policies have been introduced to support childcare and early education initiatives recently?	How have childcare and early education been influenced by recent policy?

Critical thinking has been described by Diane Halpern (1996) as:

> *thinking that is purposeful, reasoned, and goal directed – the kind of thinking involved in solving problems, formulating inferences, calculating likelihoods, and making decisions when the thinker is using skills that are thoughtful and effective.*

> (Halpern, 1996)

The emphasis is on 'thinking' that alludes to the student pausing and considering not only the topic or subject in hand, but the questions generated from taking an opportunity to ask those critical rather than factual questions.

To think critically signifies the ability to use 'a higher order skill' that enables professionals to act in a rational and reasonable manner, using empathy and understanding of others in a specific context, such as an early years setting. The rights and needs of others are always the priority, rather than blindly following established procedures.

A critical thinker:

- *raises vital questions and problems, formulating them clearly and precisely; gathers and assesses relevant information, using abstract ideas to interpret it effectively;*

- *reaches well-reasoned conclusions and solutions, testing them against relevant criteria and standards;*

- *thinks open-mindedly within alternative systems of thought, recognizing and assessing, as need be, their assumptions, implications, and practical consequences; and*

- *communicates effectively with others in figuring out solutions to complex problems.*

(Taken from Paul and Elder, 2008)

Alec Fisher (2001) examines the description given by John Dewey of what he termed '*reflective thinking as active, persistent and careful consideration of a belief or supposed form of knowledge in the light of the grounds which support it and further conclusions to which it tends*'. Rather than rushing to discover what you believe to be 'the answer', consider disentangling the question and the 'right answer' before stating your conclusion. Could there be more to find by turning your factual question into a critical question?

Below are examples of a student discussing her recent visit to another early years setting. The first question is what King (1995) describes as a factual question, and you can see we have highlighted exactly where the facts are in the answer. The second question is a critical question (King, 1995), and again we have highlighted in the answer where the critical elements are.

Question (factual)

What did you see in the new setting that is different from your setting?

> *The equipment that was out didn't seem a lot [FCT], in my setting we have everything out [FCT] so the children can access it all, you know like continuous provision. In the other setting they had bare shelves [FC] and they told me that new equipment was only brought out when the children had mastered those already out [FCT]. They didn't seem to be bothered about the EYFS either, like nothing in the planning was linked to the EYFS [FCT].*

(Early childhood studies student, 2013)

Question (critical)

Consider the two different approaches, in your setting and the one that you visited. What impact do you think they have on the children's learning and development?

> *I suppose I can see that when we put so much toys and materials out, that there are always children who get things out but don't have a clue how to use it. I guess it would be better if there was less and that the things they did get out were right for the developmental level of each child [CRIT]. I suppose this is how we interpret continuous provision [CRIT]. I think as well that the other setting were using the EYFS to measure*

the development and learning of each child [CRIT], but they knew framework and the children well enough not to have to write it all down all the time [CRIT]. They spend most of their time with the children where as we spend a lot of time sitting writing.

(Early childhood studies student, 2013)

Another example of how you can become a critical thinker might be in asking yourself critical questions as you read and research a topic.

Thought provoking or critical questions require students to go beyond the facts to think about the in ways that are different from what is presented explicitly in class or in the text.

(King, 1995, p 14)

Stella Cottrell (2005) suggests that 'one must know what we think about a subject and then be able to justify why we think in a certain way 'having reasons for what we believe...critically evaluation our own beliefs...[and be] able to present to others the reasons for our beliefs and actions' (Cottrell, 2005, p 3).

Five questions towards critical thinking

1. Do I understand what I am reading?

2. Can I explain what I have read (factually)? For example, what is this author telling me about this subject?

3. What do I think? For example, what is my standpoint, what do I believe is right?

4. Why do I think that way (critically)? For example, I think that way because I have seen this concept work in practice.

5. Can I justify to another person my way of thinking?

All that we ask is that you take the time to stop, and consider what you are reading:

What a sad comment on modern educational systems that most learners neither value nor practise active, critical reflection. They are too busy studying to stop and think.
Don't be

(Hammond and Collins, 1991, p 163)

We encourage you to take time to ask yourself, your peers and your tutors inquisitive and exploratory questions about the topic explored herein, and to stop for a while to move on from the surface level factual questioning for which you will no doubt only find factual answers, and to ponder the wider concepts, the implications to practice and to ask the searching questions to which you may not find such a concrete answer.

For as Van Gelder so eloquently suggests, learning about it is not as useful as doing it:

For students to improve, they must engage in critical thinking itself. It is not enough to learn about critical thinking. These strategies are about as effective as working on your tennis game by watching Wimbledon. Unless the students are actively doing the thinking themselves, they will never improve.

Tim (Van Gelder, 2005, p 43)

since 1988 devoted to
Critical -informal reasoning

Ben :
Australia
software

1 International perspectives on workforce development in ECEC: history, philosophy and politics

**VERITY CAMPBELL-BARR, JAN GEORGESON
AND PHILIP SELBIE**

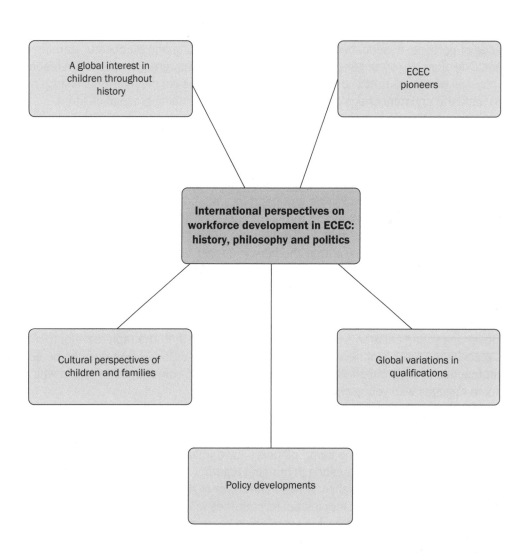

A global interest in children through history

Across the globe there is increased interest and investment in early childhood education and care. International governments (as well as supra national organisations) are increasingly recognising and valuing the role of early childhood education and care in supporting the holistic development of young children, while also acknowledging the role that early childhood education and care services have in supporting families to manage their work–life balance (particularly in relation to parental employment). Key to this interest is a growing recognition that it is not just early childhood education and care that is an important social investment tool, but *quality* early childhood education and care (Sylva et al, 2004; Lindeboom and Buiskool, 2013; Mathers and Smees, 2014). Quality is a complex term that will always be debated (Dahlberg et al, 2007; Penn, 2011), but here we are particularly interested in the role of the workforce in delivering quality early childhood education and care.

When observing an experienced early years practitioner at work with very young children it can appear almost effortless to the untrained eye. The ease with which professional and caring adults interact with the curious and often demanding needs of young children belies the daunting range of personal qualities required to create a stimulating and purposeful learning environment. Questions are often generated as fast as they are answered, emotions are responded to as physical needs are taken care of, and yet the uniqueness of the individual child is always valued amid the apparent chaos of an often noisy and demanding group of children.

ECEC pioneers

Beneath this visible surface educating and caring for very young children is a complex process. The work of an early childhood practitioner will be shaped and informed by a range of factors. Some of these factors will be grounded in a sound knowledge of early child development as well as an understanding and experience of learning theory and human relationships. This process is one that has been developed throughout history by pioneering individuals dedicated to ensuring that the very youngest in society have the best possible start to their lives. Some of these men and women held utopian dreams of social reform beginning with the wholesome education of young children, while others have had more pragmatic aims to alleviate the effects of ill health among the poor and most vulnerable (as expanded upon in Chapter 2). For some, their contribution has arisen out of a fascination with observing young children's learning in order to understand the rapid development that takes place in the first six or seven years of life. The legacy of these pioneers can be seen in the approaches to early childhood education and care that now shape the way in which the workforce engages with young children.

Throughout this book, the work of pioneering educators will be featured to consider their legacy within individual countries in shaping early childhood education and care provision and the workforce within it. Often the same pioneers have influenced practice in more than one country, but what has been interesting in bringing together a collection of chapters that span the globe is that, while individual countries might refer to the same pioneers, their interpretations can be very different. In other instances countries will have their own personal pioneers who are little recognised elsewhere, but yet they are key to the development of early childhood

[handwritten: Influence from outside factors?]

services within their homeland. What these variations in interpretation of theory and philosophy show us is that in each country a process of interpretation takes place as practitioners work out the best way to work with the youngest members of their particular society.

Cultural perspectives of children and families

The process of formulating an understanding of how to engage and work with children will reflect historical conceptions of the child and childhood. At times these conceptual features will interplay with the theoretical ideas of the pioneers, but there will be a number of other cultural forces at play. Key to the process of interpreting the knowledge that exists around early childhood education and care services is recognising that the ways in which children and childhood are viewed within a society will shape and inform what a country sees as good and appropriate experiences for them. There can be a tendency to assume that the 'natural' experience for a child's early years is to be nurtured and cared for by his/her mother, but the study of family structures over time shows that this ideal of a warm, close, intimate relationship between mother and child has not been a constant feature of children's lives (Hays, 1996) and indeed the whole idea of mothering has always been a 'contested terrain' (Glenn, 1994, p 2). The interplay between the roles of mothers, fathers and the extended family and societal structures to support the care and development of children is different in different cultures, and has changed over time. Indeed, the child's very presence in the home or outside the home at particular points in their life can signal different things in different contexts; think of the child cared for at home today by a stay-at-home mother or stay-at-home father, in comparison with the home-schooled child; each case comes with cultural baggage about what is the expected place for the child or parent, and the structures within society to support that expected solution. *[handwritten: parents needing wanting to work.]*

In most of the countries in this book, the child's developmental pathway follows a trajectory from home to daycare/nursery/kindergarten and then to school (Hedegaard and Fleer, 2008, p 11) and we can be so familiar with this that it can take on a kind of inevitability, a 'taken-for-grantedness' that masks the fact that it is a societal practice shaped by past history and current pragmatics. An early years workforce is needed now (and has been since the onset of the Industrial Revolution) so that young children can be placed in settings outside the home for part of the working day. Leaving aside for the moment why we might want to do this, it can be insightful to look at cultures or times in history with different arrangements: children have been sent away from their mothers for basic care (wet nursing); children might stay with their mothers and siblings until they are assigned work roles in the community; children are raised together in kibbutz. Thinking about other ways like these of raising children helps us to understand that present day attendance at day nursery (or other settings) is just the way childcare is arranged. Who gets to work with children outside – or inside – the home is also the result of cultural decision-making over time in the context of the pattern of jobs, qualities, qualifications and remunerations in society at large.

Critical questions

Consider the different environments where children are being cared for and educated.

» *Do the adults in these environments require qualifications?*

» *Who has determined whether they require (or not) these qualifications?*

» *Have there been any changes in history as to the requirement for qualifications?*

If we see development as '*the person's evolving conception of the ecological environment, and his [sic] relation to it, as well as the person's growing capacity to discover, sustain, alter its properties*' (Bronfenbrenner, 1979, p 9), then the environment where children spend their growing years will play an important role in their development. When children are involved in setting-based care, they are acquiring culturally appropriate knowledge by participating in an environment where they can interact with objects and routines from the 'nursery treasure chest' (Georgeson, 2009). Here we understand culture as '*the entire pool of artifacts (including language, norms, customs, tools, values) accumulated by the social group in the course of its historical experience*' (Cole and Hatano, 2007, p 111).

Policy developments

One aspect that will shape what counts as appropriate environments for young children is the history of the country, possibly linked to the individual pioneers who lived or travelled there, but also the historical interest in early childhood services. A key aspect of the historical interest is the extent to which policymakers have taken an interest in early childhood services. This will shape how particular societies see the role of early childhood practitioners, and the differential weights given to the complementary roles of education and caring. Indeed in recent times other roles have accrued: an early childhood practitioner might now also be expected to take the role of supporting and educating parents as well as children, as governments proclaim the importance of good parenting and seek ways to support those parents whose behaviours do not correspond to ideals.

As we look around the globe we can see some very clear differences in how early childhood services have been supported. Differences lie in the level of funding allocated by individual governments to early childhood services, whether the funding comes from central or local government, the composition of the different types of institutions available (such as preschool, kindergarten, day nursery), the market structure (such as all state provision or a mixed market approach), not to mention the qualification requirements. Increasingly, policymakers have taken an interest in the provision of early childhood education and care services, and often the result is that they become involved in moulding the early childhood education and care provision to fit their ideological position. The development of curriculum documents, qualifications structures and requirements and minimum quality standards will all form a process of shaping early childhood education and care provision. In the chapters that follow we can see the influence of policymakers, but we can also identify that there are different approaches and therefore experiences. For example, Sweden is an example of a country where there has been relatively early policy interest in the role that early childhood education and care services can play in the wider social welfare structure. This is contrasted with a country such as the Philippines that is still in the early stages of developing policy in the field of early childhood education and care. Hungary offers an example of where early childhood education and care providers are offered relative autonomy in their approach, when contrasted to the heavily regulated systems that are present in the UK.

The historical policy developments around early childhood education and care provision are important as past political decisions will have a bearing on the direction of future policy developments. Path dependency reflects that decisions in the present can often be limited by those of the past. This can be because it is just easier to continue along the same path or because it is more cost effective. While in some cases this may enable robust early childhood education and care services and structures to develop, with a strong sense of tradition, in other cases it can feel like being stuck in a rut, with a lack of innovation. The latter can have implications for the early childhood education and care workforce, since though they might crave change, such as higher level qualifications, they can often be restricted by the political structures around them (see Osgood, 2010).

Global variations in qualifications

Key to this book we also see a number of contrasting ideas around the nature of the early childhood education and care workforce. One aspect of this is the level of qualifications required to work in early childhood education and care services, with variations existing both across and within countries. Qualification requirements can vary as a result of the type of early childhood education and care setting and the age of the child being cared for. Qualifications will also vary in terms of the level (further education, higher education, Master's) and the duration of the course, not to mention the content of the course. Increasingly, questions are being asked about the knowledge and skills required of the workforce, the role do attitudinal competences play in the skill set needed to work with young children and how to teach and/or develop these in early childhood education and care practitioners (CoRe, 2011)? Such questions highlight that the role of an early childhood practitioner is a complex one.

Critical questions

»   What do you consider to be the knowledge, skills and attitudinal competences to work with young children?

»   Where do you feel you learn about these – through training, while in practice, from your family?

What is also apparent is that there is a complex array of terms used to describe those who work with young children. To some extent the terms used reflect how the purpose of early childhood education and care has been constructed in relation to the needs of the child. At this simplest level this is a difference between education-based terms, such as the Early Years Teacher, care-based terms, such as a Nursery Assistant, and those that look to blend together these two aspects, such as the Early Childhood Pedagogue. However, it is clear that in recent years the terminology to describe those who work with young children increasingly reflects a structural process of meeting standards and demonstrating specific areas of knowledge. Decisions about the skill set required of those working in early childhood education and care have become a top-down political process in many countries, embedded in increasingly bureaucratic procedures. Our fear is that some of the key features of the philosophical approaches that you will see in this book might be reduced to a series of assessment criteria. We also have concerns that while it might appear relatively straightforward to determine the knowledge and skills required, assessing emotional competence is something that is a challenge for policymakers. The result is that emotional indicators can be ignored, despite their importance to the individuals who choose to enter the early childhood education and care workforce.

Critical reflections

As will be seen in the chapters of this book, being a part of the early childhood education and care workforce involves a complex mix of historical ideas around children and childhood and political perspectives on the role and function of early childhood education and care services. As a member of the early childhood education and care workforce you will find yourself negotiating between the historical, philosophical and political perspectives that are present within and beyond your home country. The chapters in this book are designed to enable you to think about what shapes your role as an early childhood practitioner, to consider how your experiences are similar to those of practitioners in other countries, to recognise how your thoughts and beliefs about early childhood education and care service are representative of those in other countries and to maybe even want to travel to see first-hand what working in early childhood education and care is like in another country. Ultimately, considering your experiences and beliefs enables you to critically reflect on your own practice. To ask questions of why you approach your work in the way that you do and to feel confident in your emerging understanding of who you are as a practitioner is always an ongoing process, but one that is shaped by your own history, philosophy and politics.

Further reading

Nutbrown, C, Clough, P and Selbie, P (2008) *Early Childhood Education: History, Philosophy and Experience*. London: Sage.

This is a really valuable book for considering in more detail the history and philosophy of early childhood education and care practices. The authors offer overviews of the pioneers that we will encounter in this book – and more. Through tracing the pioneers in history, the authors identify common themes that can be seen as guiding the provision of early childhood education and care services, such as play, children's rights and early intervention. A second edition is now available.

Oberhuemer, P, Schreyer, I and Neuman, M (2010) *Professionals in Early Childhood Education and Care Systems: European Profiles and Perspectives*. Leverkusen Opladen: Barbra Budich Publishers.

This is a useful book as it offers chapters that present an overview of the early childhood education and care workforce in several countries. It is a useful reference tool in providing an understanding of what the requirements that different countries have for their early childhood education and care workforce are. There is also some consideration of key changes in history and policy within countries.

Tomlinson, P (2013) *Early Years Policy and Practice: A Critical Alliance*. Northwich: Critical Publishing.

A comprehensive and up-to-date critique of national and international political, economic and social agendas that influence children's lives and early years professional practice.

References

Bronfenbrenner, U (1979) *The Ecology of Human Development: Experiments by Nature and Design*. Cambridge, MA: Harvard University Press.

Cole, M and Hatano, G (2007) Cultural-Historical Activity Theory: Integrating Phylogeny, Cultural History, and Ontogenesis in Cultural Psychology, in Kitayama, S and Cohen, D (eds) *Handbook of Cultural Psychology*. New York: Guilford Press, pp 109–35.

CoRe (2011) Competence Requirements in Early Childhood Education and Care: A Study for the European Commission Directorate-General for Education and Culture, University of East London and University of Ghent: London. [online] Available at: http://ec.europa.eu/education/more-information/doc/2011/core_en.pdf (accessed 11 September 2013).

Dahlberg, G, Moss, P and Pence, A (2007) *Beyond Quality in Early Childhood Education and Care: Languages of Evaluation* (2nd edn). London: Falmer Press.

Georgeson, J M (2009) The Professionalisation of the Early Years Workforce, in Edwards, S and Nuttall, J (eds) *Professional Learning in Early Childhood Settings*. Rotterdam: Sense.

Glenn, E N (1994) Social Constructions of Mothering: A Thematic Overview, in Glenn, E N, Chang, G and Forcey, L R (eds) *Mothering, Ideology, Experience and Agency*. London: Routledge.

Hays, S (1996) *The Cultural Contradictions of Mothering*. Connecticut: Yale University Press.

Hedegaard, M and Fleer, M (2008) *Studying Children: A Cultural-Historical Approach*. Maidenhead: Open University Press.

Lindeboom, G and Buiskool, B (2013) *Quality in Early Childhood Education and Care: Annex Report Country and Case Studies*. Directorate-General for International Policies, Policy Department: European Parliament.

Mathers, S and Smees, R (2014) Quality and Inequality: Do Three- and Four-Year-Olds in Deprived Areas Experience Lower Quality Early Years Provision? Nuffield Foundation. [online] Available at: www.nuffieldfoundation.org/sites/default/files/files/Quality_inequality_childcare_mathers_29_05_14.pdf (accessed 28 November 2014).

Osgood, J (2010) Reconstructing Professionalism in ECEC: The Case for the 'Critically Reflective Emotional Professional'. *Early Years: An International Journal of Research and Development*, 30(2): 119–33.

Penn, H (2011) *Quality in Early Childhood Services*. McGraw-Hill: Berkshire.

Sylva, K, Melhuish, T, Sammons, P, Siraj-Blatchford, I and Taggart, B (2004) *The Effective Provision of Pre-School Education (EPPE) Project: Final Report*. A Longitudinal Study Funded by the DfES 1997–2004. Nottingham: DfES.

Part A
Philosophical pioneers

2 Britain: a complex mix of philosophy and politics

**PHILIP SELBIE, LYNN BLAKEMORE, CLAIRE FARLEY
AND VERITY CAMPBELL-BARR**

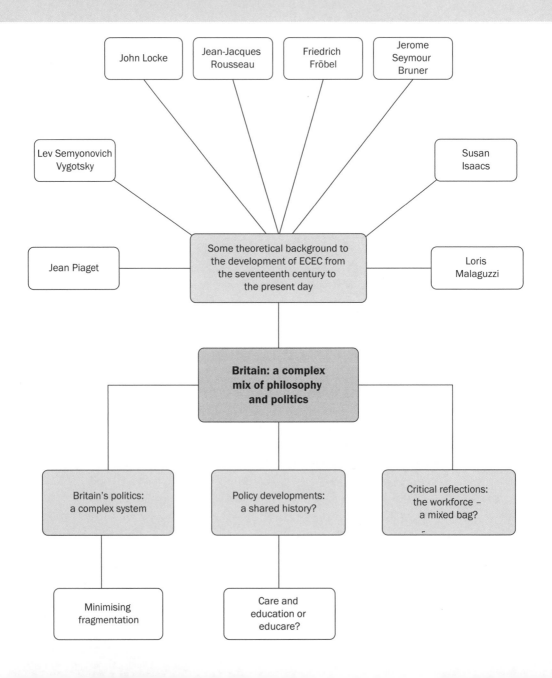

Introduction

This chapter explores the complex picture of early childhood education and care (ECEC) in Britain. The chapter begins with an exploration of the philosophies (and the pioneers) that have influenced approaches to working with children in the British context. Many of these pioneers represent the philanthropic history of ECEC provision in Britain. Pioneers have generally been selected as particular proponents of theories relating to young children's early learning rather than as the first or most well-known figure in history. Yet while there is a common collection of ideas behind the provision of ECEC that can be traced through history, policy developments cannot be characterised in the same way. The nature of British politics and the lack of political interest in ECEC until relatively recently means that ECEC in Britain is characterised by fragmentation. Throughout the chapter we draw on case studies from the countries that form Britain. However, they are illustrative rather than exhaustive, and we recognise their limitations. For the sake of clarity, we refer to ECEC, but recognise (and later consider) the debates around the relationship between care and education in the British approach.

Some theoretical background to the development of ECEC from the seventeenth century to the present day

Understanding how to educate and care for very young children is a complex process based upon knowledge of child development as well as understanding of learning theory tested within the crucible of human relationships. The process is one that has developed through history by pioneering individuals dedicated to ensuring the very youngest in society have the best possible start to their lives. Some of these men and women had utopian dreams of social reform being rooted in the education of young children, such as Jan Amos Comenius (1592–1670), who referred to schools as 'the workshops of humanity' (1636, p 223). Others have had more pragmatic aims of alleviating the effects of ill health among the poor, such as Margaret McMillan (1860–1931), who began her work with the most vulnerable by opening her Deptford nursery school in Southeast London. Believing that a rich and healthy outdoor learning environment was for all children, she declared that *'the best classroom and the richest cupboard are roofed only by the sky'*. For some, their contribution derives from a fascination with observing young children's learning to understand the rapid development that takes place in the early years of human life. The following discussion of the pioneers offers understanding of what (and who) has influenced and shaped the development of high quality provision with young children in Britain today. We see common themes in their ideas that still hold significance today, as we will see at the end of the chapter.

John Locke - 1632 - 1704

Well-known for his belief that newborn children were akin to a *blank slate* (*tabula rasa*), John Locke (1632–1704) believed that for the child to lead a good and virtuous life the teacher's role was to write whatever was necessary for that purpose. Although he devoted the major part of his great treatise *Some Thoughts Concerning Education* (1693) to this idea, Locke also made clear his conviction that experience was the greatest teacher of all. He saw no reason why learning should not be enjoyable and the outcome of exploration, discovery and playful interaction with the world. Locke was an advocate of clear boundaries in order to help children gradually master their childish passions by appealing to their rational minds. Furthermore, he did not advocate physical punishment and suggested that young children should remain with their parents who were best placed to model good examples for their children to follow. Originally written for an aristocratic friend, *Some Thoughts Concerning Education* soon became popular with a wider audience who saw the merits of education as a means to character formation.

Jean-Jacques Rousseau

Jean-Jacques Rousseau (1712–78) also proposed that young children's natural disposition to explore should be encouraged. Rousseau's ideas became the basis for a fictional work entitled *Emile: Or on Education* (1762) in which he set out how a child should be educated from infancy to adulthood. The teacher in 'Emile' stands back and allows the child to direct his own learning instead of playing a more active part in guiding the child's learning as proposed 70 years earlier by Locke. Rousseau's belief in the inherent goodness of children aligned him closely with the Romanticism of the first half of the nineteenth century when, somewhat as a reaction against the harsh realities of the Industrial Revolution, children were to be protected and treasured for their state of innocence (see Gabriel, 2010). Rousseau and his contemporaries saw education's priority as one of drawing upon the potential that nature had already placed within the child rather than to emphasise the role of the all-knowing teacher.

Similar to Locke, Rousseau favoured the use of sensory training and the enjoyment of natural objects rather than traditional schooling based upon the study of symbols. However, in a marked contrast to his predecessor, Rousseau's Romantic inclinations led him to believe that ultimately education of the very young was the basis for reforming society rather than simply shaping the growing infant into adulthood.

Friedrich Fröbel   ·1782–1852

Another pioneer pre-occupied with the purpose of education was Friedrich Fröbel (1782–1852), who also recognised the importance of nature in educating young children. As outlined by Hohmann, in Chapter 8, Fröbel was a strong advocate of play and believed in self-initiated activities as the best means to effective learning for young children. He also advocated the importance of objects to support the process of early learning, designing and making ten special resources which he called 'gifts'. Each set of 'gifts' was designed to be used with certain materials and in specific ways which he called 'occupations', such as threading beads, folding paper or moulding clay to encourage manipulative development. Fröbel noticed young children's instinctive desire to build and construct and so he developed the 'gifts' and 'occupations' not just to provide sensory experience of the material world but also to give young minds an insight into more abstract and philosophical concepts such as the interconnectivity of human relationships. Fröbel opened his first kindergarten in 1839 based upon his belief that it should represent an extension of the home where children would be cultivated rather than coerced into learning. Alongside this, children would be provided with plenty of outdoor space to observe the natural world, follow their intuition and develop their physical capabilities in an atmosphere of freedom reminiscent of the experiential learning espoused by Locke and echoing the Romanticism of Rousseau.

Lev Semyonovich Vygotsky

Observing the effect of young children's natural inclination to play and form relationships with others was one of the major influences upon the work of arguably the most important developmental psychologist of the early twentieth century: Lev Semyonovich Vygotsky (1896–1934). As considered in detail by Murphy and Hayes (in Chapter 3) Vygotsky's ideas included his concept of the 'zone of proximal development' (ZPD), associated with the idea that young children's abilities are best developed in collaboration with others. According to Vygotsky, learning occurs in this zone and it is not difficult to observe this theory evident in early learning today as a skilled practitioner watches children discovering the limits to their ability and intuitively knows when to stand back and when to sensitively support a child's learning to the next level.

Jerome Seymour Bruner

Several decades after Vygotsky, Jerome Seymour Bruner (1915–) also argued against the idea that children learn in isolation; instead they develop a framework for thinking through working with others in a cultural context. It is in this context that Bruner gave rise to the term 'scaffolding' and developed further the image of the learner being supported through the ZPD when his or her independent efforts prove insufficient. Taking the analogy of a building one stage further, Bruner suggested that a metaphorical scaffold not only provides a foothold for the child to reach a new next level, but it also acts as a stabilising mechanism in times of doubt and insecurity until it is time for it to be withdrawn.

Susan Isaacs

Close observations of young children's learning became a feature of the work of Susan Isaacs (1885–1948) at the experimental Malting House School in Cambridge where she took up the post of principal in 1924. Isaacs believed in child-centred learning and saw the nursery school as a place that provided social experiences and friendships – things she considered vital for children's early learning and development. Isaacs expanded upon Fröbel and McMillan's approach to active learning in the outdoors despite some criticism rooted in the social climate of the period.

Similar to Vygotsky before and others after her, Isaacs believed that knowledge about children came from observing them, and so she produced record cards for teachers to use which were designed to build up a picture of the whole child. However, as well as encouraging a more studied approach, Isaacs also encouraged the teacher to enter the world of children and participate in their play to encourage the imagination as well as the development of physical and cognitive skills. She fervently believed that the early years setting should be an extension of the home and mirror the function of the family through love and warmth but it should also offer new opportunities and exciting resources that might not be available at home.

Indeed, times were changing and society was beginning to get used to the concept of equal opportunities, not just for men and women, rich and poor but for children too. During much of the nineteenth century, the pioneers working with young children were motivated by the belief that education was no longer purely for the privileged few but should be available for everyone and it must begin with the very young. At the same time ECEC was becoming much more established as taking place outside the home environment although Isaacs was careful to ensure that those working with her did not neglect the important role played by parents as well as the environment within the home itself.

Loris Malaguzzi

Over time, influences from ECEC practice in other parts of the world have begun to shape the character of ECEC in Britain. It is unwise to believe the success of working in a particular way with children in one culture can be authentically reproduced in another; however, the work of Loris Malaguzzi (1920–94) has spread across the world in recent years. In Chapter 4, Caruso and Sorzio discuss developments in the North Italian region of Emilia-Romagna. Malaguzzi believed in the importance of the early years of life as a time when children form their own personality and learn together as part of a community. He believed in the importance of exploration and discovery for young children and that children express themselves in a multiplicity of ways (as Malaguzzi claimed, in the 'hundred languages' of the child). Today Reggio Emilia preschools and those inspired by them (including in Britain) view their children as competent and capable in their own right and also acknowledge that while they learn most successfully in partnership with others, learning is most effective within a rich stimulating environment which Malaguzzi referred to as 'the third educator'.

Influences from overseas have also seen a relatively recent emphasis on outdoor learning with the rise in popularity of Forest Schools. Margaret McMillan and her sister Rachel McMillan (1859–1917) certainly recognised the value of the outdoors for young children's health and well-being. However, using the outdoors as the principal environment for learning probably has its roots in the work of Fröbel. The Danish approach to outdoor education caught the attention of early years practitioners in this country towards the end of the twentieth century and young children then began to benefit from a very rich experience of learning in all weathers and temperatures using sticks, mud, knives and fire. There is no doubt that Forest Schools have drawn attention once again to the potential of the natural environment for learning which in turn has (re)introduced practitioners to the benefits of experiencing risk for young children's personal as well as cognitive development.

Jean Piaget

In recognising the importance of the early years for cognitive development, we must acknowledge that increasingly ECEC has become about just this. As in Hungary (see Chapter 9), psychology and theories of child development have often moulded the character and purpose of ECEC; their application to working with children to support their development is a contested area. In recent times perhaps the differences of opinion have been most notable when the highly influential theories of Jean Piaget (1896–1980) were challenged by one of his co-workers. Margaret Donaldson (1926–) published her ground-breaking book '*Children's Minds*' in 1978 in which she argued that Piaget's theories on the developmental stages of children were too rigid and that his experiments had significant limitations. Donaldson's views at the time were widely regarded as a necessary corrective to the more extreme inter-pretations of Piaget's theories about children's early development. Piaget concluded that during what he termed the pre-operational stage of cognitive development, children could not yet see things from another or different point of view, which had widespread implications for education. Donaldson suggested that by the age of three most children were quite cap-able of doing this provided they had appropriate contextual cues.

Critical questions

Reflect back on the different pioneers that have featured in this chapter so far.

» *Which of the pioneers did you identify with?*

» *What did you like about their approach to working with children?*

» *Why do you like this particular approach?*

In many respects we have ended where we began by recognising the centrality of the child in the theories proposed by some of the pioneers of early childhood education over the last 350 years. The philosophical legacy of these pioneers is evident in current ECEC practice in Britain which suggests that there is a common core that has shaped ways of working with young children in Britain. We will now turn our attention to politics to see whether the com-monality remains.

Britain's politics: a complex system

It is not uncommon for the United Kingdom (UK) and Britain to be used interchangeably. Indeed, there are even occasions where England is used as being synonymous with either/ or the UK and Britain. The UK has devolved many political responsibilities to the four nations that form it, but we should be mindful that a focus on *Britain* and the idea of a *British* approach should also take into account other regions, including Jersey and Guernsey which, although never devolved, are dependencies of the British Crown and add to the complexities of political systems.

Devolution is designed to decentralise government by allocating more powers to the four nations which form the UK: England, Northern Ireland, Scotland and Wales. Under devolution each of these countries has the power (and responsibility) to make policy decisions. However, the extent of devolution varies between countries, with Scotland having more devolved pow-ers than Wales and Northern Ireland; it has responsibility for more areas and can create legislation. For all nations education (including ECEC and the ECEC workforce) is devolved; for Jersey and Guernsey, however, the relationship is somewhat different.

CASE STUDY

Jersey, a small state

Jersey is a parliamentary democracy that is a dependency of the British Crown. It is a British island, but it is not part of the United Kingdom. The Island is not a full member of the EU but has a special relationship and maintains some benefits through protocol 3. The Island's link with the United Kingdom and the rest of the Commonwealth is through Her Majesty Queen Elizabeth II, who as the Sovereign is the Head of State; however, within the Island the Sovereign is represented by the Lieutenant Governor with whom official relations and communications take place (States of Jersey, 2008). The Island's parliament is the States of Jersey, consisting of 53 elected members from a range of island-wide and parochial constituencies. The States is divided into ten departments, with each one of them having a minister and assistant minister. Departments deal with different sides of Island life including health, education and economic development. Remaining States members include a Chief Minister who presides over the whole of the States and various scrutiny panels who monitor and supervise States policies (States of Jersey, 2008).

Acts of the Westminster Parliament do not apply routinely to the Island, although occasionally mainland legislation does include the Island directly but with amendments as may be deemed necessary by the States of Jersey to reflect Island culture. By convention, the United Kingdom has assumed responsibility for the Island's foreign affairs but, even in those matters, the United Kingdom again only acts with the approval of the States of Jersey. Consequently, the States can, and frequently does, legislate independently to implement international agreements (States of Jersey, 2008). As a result of being a micro-climate, parallels with the UK cannot be drawn and paradoxically, even compared to Guernsey, as another Peculiar of the Crown, the differences are still very apparent.

Minimising fragmentation

The picture for Britain is therefore one where Jersey, for example, has a history of independence, whereas Scotland has devolved responsibility (although, following a vote on independence where Scotland decided to remain part of the UK, Scotland's devolved responsibilities are being reviewed). Consequently Acts of Parliament that come through Westminster do not routinely apply, which explains why Acts often refer to England and Wales but not other parts of Britain.

Policy design and approach to ECEC are therefore fragmented but the British government (via Westminster) still seeks to influence these devolved powers and, to a certain extent, control them (Wincott, 2005). This can be done via allocation of resources from the Treasury, but there is also an expectation that all nations forming Britain will uphold the core policy objectives of the Party(s) in power. However, detail about how each nation meets policy objectives can vary. For example, there are Childcare Strategies across all of the nations stemming from the 1998 Green Paper: *Meeting the Childcare Challenge* (DfEE, 1998), which included a focus on up-skilling the ECEC workforce that is still present today, most recently evident in

More Great Childcare (DfE, 2013). However, in each nation the nature of the qualifications required and curriculum followed by staff varies.

Critical questions

» *What do you think of the devolved model?*

» *Do you think it is right and appropriate for each nation to be able to adapt national (core policies) to reflect the local context? Why do you think this?*

» *Do you think there is a role for Westminster in still determining a common core for the policy developments of ECEC? Why?*

Policy developments: a shared history?

Although we suggest a common core to policy developments in ECEC in Britain, policy interest in ECEC has not always been present. Early developments of ECEC services were motivated by philanthropists, often community focused (Payler et al, 2013). Just as the pioneers who we have outlined earlier in this chapter were motivated by meeting the educational needs and supporting the well-being of children, so too were these philanthropists. Political interest in ECEC was often a response to philanthropic concerns or because ECEC served a particular need, such as supporting the war effort during World War II. Following the war, policymakers largely ignored ECEC with most nurseries closing (Randall, 2000) and the care of young children promoted as a family (primarily a maternal) matter. The return of women to the home has been attributed to interpretations of Bowlby's Maternal Attachment Theory, which emphasised the importance of maternal care following the large scale evacuations that had occurred during the war. This was also consistent with the economic need to ensure jobs were available for men, but the closures have also been attributed to the health and hygiene of nurseries at the time (Randall, 2000).

The period following promoted the male breadwinner model, whereby women stayed at home and cared for children, with the state only intervening at times when a family was deemed 'in need'. With mothers caring for their children there was no need for (or interest in) ECEC. While a few parliamentary reports, such as the Plowden Report in 1967, signalled some policy interest in ECEC provision, there were few actual developments. The result was a patchwork of ECEC provision across Britain; some local authority areas put ECEC in place to support vulnerable families, while others relied on local community groups or entrepreneurs to meet local demand.

During the 1980s, despite growing demand for childcare as maternal employment increased, the government maintained that ECEC was a private matter for families (see Campbell-Barr, 2010). In the 1990s, the then Conservative government began to offer some support for out-of-school childcare and introduced the Childcare Disregard for low-income families. In 1996 a Nursery Voucher scheme was introduced, but was doomed to failure due to a lack of ECEC places.

Care and education or educare?

Since 1997 and the election of New Labour, policy for ECEC has seen rapid developments and (compared to what had gone before) considerable investment (see Tomlinson, 2013). Under the devolved Childcare Strategies, the government looked to expand the level of provision, support the cost of accessing services and improve the quality (including revising qualifications of the ECEC workforce). However, while provision includes both education and care – educare – their relationship in policy development has been far from straightforward. Funding arrangements vary between education and care services; early years education is a state entitlement, but childcare is subsidised for low-income families (although with subtle variations across Britain).

CASE STUDY

Northern Ireland and ECEC

Northern Ireland has increased the supply of part-time early education provision, with government funding for part-time places (primarily in the voluntary and private sectors). Early years education is not a state entitlement, but the government is looking to provide a year of preschool for every child (with children starting school at four years of age). The Department of Education aims to create a strategy to combine care and education for children from birth to six years of age (see Eurodyce at NFER, 2009).

Historically there were also differences in the curriculum and registration processes for early years education and childcare providers. Ultimately, early years education was about early intervention and child development, while childcare met the needs of working parents. Childcare became associated with those under three and early years education with three- and four-years-olds in preschool. This division was criticised for ignoring the practice and theory behind both education and care which reflected an approach that combined the two elements (see Bennett, 2003; Moss, 2006).

Criticisms of the split system led each part of Britain to consider ways in which they might create a more holistic approach. Often this meant reconsidering the scope of the curriculum; for example, England combined Birth to Three Matters and the Foundation Stage (see Brooker, 2014) to form the Early Years Foundation Stage (DfE, 2014). Wales has the Foundation Phase, covering children from three to seven years of age and Scotland has the Curriculum for Excellence, which covers children from three to eighteen years of age.

CASE STUDY

The Scottish Curriculum

The Curriculum for Excellence applies to children aged 3 to 18, but is divided into two aspects: A Curriculum Framework for children 3 to 5 and the 5 to 14 curriculum.

The Curriculum for Excellence focuses on:

- active, experiential learning;
- a holistic approach to learning;
- smooth transitions; and
- learning through play.

The intention is that these principles will carry through to practice beyond the early years.

Critical questions

» *When you think about your own work with children, do you view it as care, education or educare?*

» *Do you think policy has shaped your thinking in any way or has it come from theory (thinking back to the pioneers)?*

» *How would you like to see policy develop in the future, for example equal funding, a revised curriculum?*

Other efforts to combine care and education are evident in developing a combined registration process. To be eligible for funding and for parents to be able to draw down tax credits to support the cost of childcare, providers are required to register with the relevant body (each part of Britain has its own version). The registration process is a political tool for monitoring and regulating activities of ECEC providers in a mixed market model. The mixed market model is a characteristic feature of ECEC provision across Britain (see Penn, 2012); when the National Childcare Strategy looked to expand the level of ECEC provision, it was clear that the focus would be on the market (not the state) to do this (Campbell-Barr, 2014).

CASE STUDY

Regulating a mixed market: comparing England and Jersey

There are some historical similarities in the regulation of ECEC in England and Jersey, but one major element in the structure of the legislation is different. A local adjustment to the Children Act (1948) had to acknowledge the Committee system of government on the Island; responsibilities of the Education Committee are therefore defined in Article 68, by empowering the Committee to '*determine requirements in connexion with registration*' (Mountford, 2004). What this means in legislative and administrative terms is that once the regulatory requirements are agreed by a democratic consensus of Committee members, this lays down the conditions for registration of private sector childcare provision, and thus the administrative responsibilities of the Committee's officers. The strength of this structure is that it has the potential for review and changes can be made without recourse to expensive and lengthy legislative reform.

Despite similarities between Jersey and England, policy for registration in Jersey has increasingly diverged from the regulatory framework in England (Mountford, 2004). The introduction of the Office for Standards in Education (Ofsted) as the registration body in England in 1999 removed the delegated responsibility for regulation from local authority level to a centralised (and more bureaucratic) administration. In contrast, the partnership between provider and regulator in Jersey has become more collaborative, although further scrutiny is needed as the regulatory process is operated by a small team of regulators who are in effect unregulated themselves.

Critical reflections: the workforce – a mixed bag?

ECEC in Britain is something of a mixed bag. As we have seen there is more than one curriculum and registering body across Britain. The case study from Jersey suggests that this form of fragmentation could be a good thing as it enables possibilities to create local solutions to local problems. In the case of Jersey, the relative small geographical area of the Island means that engagement with local politicians is a reality for ECEC providers on the Island. However, contrast this with the larger area of England or Scotland (with some communities on islands off the North coast of the mainland) – what opportunities do practitioners here have for engaging with policymakers? One of the key criticisms of the National Childcare Strategy is that it has been done to ECEC providers, rather than with them (McGillivray, 2008). Jersey offers an alternative perspective. Lundy (2007) has praised the system for producing critically reflective practitioners, rather than a system where providers fear being blamed for their mistakes, as is evident in England.

In considering the workforce it is impossible not to reflect on the consequences of the mixed market model for those working in ECEC in Britain. As a member of the ECEC workforce, you can be responsible for delivering the same curriculum and being subject to scrutiny by the same regulatory body as the setting down the road; those working in the maintained sector will be qualified teachers (at degree level), be on a national pay scale and are often represented by unions. Practitioners in the, private, voluntary and independent (PVI) sectors, however, will range from having no qualifications to having a degree, receive variable levels of pay and while numerous national organisations seek to represent these workers, they are not represented by a union. The result is the workforce is incredibly mixed, both regarding level of qualifications held by practitioners, the method of undertaking qualifications (work-based or college-/university-based) and the content and structure of provision. This variation was recently criticised in the Nutbrown Review (DfE, 2012) concerning both the range of qualifications that exist, and also their fitness for purpose.

This fragmentation could paint a bleak picture of Britain, or prompt celebration of its diversity. We return to the pioneers that we considered at the outset of this chapter. Throughout Britain, those working in ECEC hold strong beliefs about the fundamental importance of play in the early years as a method of learning, the significance of the outdoors as an environment for supporting children's development and the pivotal role of adults in scaffolding children's learning. In many respects this reflects their child-centred approach – one that advocates listening to the child and acting on their interests. To do this, there is a long and strong history of using observations to inform practice. As a sector, there may be political debates and fragmented policy decisions, but the workforce shares a common set of philosophies that they adapt to fit the needs of the children they work with.

Further reading

Tomlinson, P (2013) *Early Years Policy and Practice: A Critical Alliance*. Northwich: Critical Publishing.

The first chapter of this book offers some more detail on the historical developments of ECEC and the interplay that they have with some of the pioneers who we have detailed here.

Wincott, D (2004) Devolution, Social Democracy and Policy Diversity in Britain: The Case of Childcare and Early Years Policies. [online] Available at: www.ippr.org/assets/media/uploadedFiles/ippr-north/events/2004/sem1-paper%20on%20childcare.pdf (accessed 14 August 2014).

Devolution is difficult to understand and we have only touched the surface here. In this paper Wincott considers in detail Devolution in the UK. Interestingly many of the developments that took place in the 2000s for ECEC ran alongside the devolution process, so often ECEC was subject to competing agendas.

References

Bennett, J (2003) Starting Strong. *Journal of Early Childhood Research*, 1(1): 21–48.

Brooker, L (2014) An Overview of Early Education in England, in Moyles, J, Payler, J and Georgeson, J (eds) *Early Years Foundations: Critical Issues*. Maidenhead: McGraw Hill.

Campbell-Barr, V (2010) The Research, Policy and Practice Triangle in Early Childhood Education and Care, in Parker-Rees, Leeson, Willan and Savage, *Early Childhood Studies: An Introduction to the Study of Children's Lives and World*. 3rd edn. Exeter: Learning Matters.

Campbell-Barr, V (2014) Constructions of Early Childhood Education and Care Provision: Negotiating Discourses. *Contemporary Issues in Early Childhood*, 15(1): 5–17.

Comenius, J A (1896) *The Great Didactic*. (M Keatinge, trans). London: A & C Black (original work published in 1636).

DfE (Department for Education) (2012) *Foundations for Quality: The Independent Review of Early Education and Childcare Qualifications (Final Report)*. Runcorn: Department for Education.

DfE (Department for Education) (2013) *More Great Childcare*. London: Crown Copyright.

DfEE (Department for Education and Employment) (1998) *Meeting the Childcare Challenge: A Consultation Document*. London: Crown Copyright.

DfE (Department for Education) (2014) *Statutory Framework for the Early Years Foundation Stage*. London: Department for Education.

Donaldson, M (1976) *Children's Minds*. London: Fontana.

Eurodyce at NFER (2009) *Early Childhood Education and Care in Europe*.

Fröbel, F (1887) *The Education of Man*. (W N Hailmann, trans). New York, NY: D Appleton Century (Original work published in 1826).

Gabriel, N (2010) Adults' Concepts of Childhood, in Parker-Rees R, Leeson C (eds) *Early Childhood Studies: An Introduction to the Study of Children's Worlds and Children's Lives*, Exeter: Learning Matters pp 137–151.

Locke, J (1963) *Some Thoughts Concerning Education*. Heinemann: London (original work published in 1692).

Lundy, M (2007) *Education and Home Affairs Scrutiny Panel Early Years*. States of Jersey.

McGillivray, G (2008) Nannies, Nursery Nurses and Early Years Professionals: Constructions of Professional Identity in the Early Years Workforce in England. *European Early Childhood Education Research Journal*, 16(2): 242–54.

Moss, P (2006) Farwell to Childcare? *National Institute Economic Review*, 195: 70–83.

Mountford, S (2004) Raising the Quality of Registered Day Care in the Micro-State of Jersey, Influencing Policy and Practice, Unpublished PhD thesis, Institute of Education University College Worcester.

Payler, J, Georgeson, J and Wickett, K (2013) Early Childhood Education and Care in the UK: Piecemeal Development through Philanthropy, Propagation, Pluralism and Pragmatism, in Georgeson, J and Payler, J (eds) *International Perspectives on Early Childhood Education and Care*. Maindenhead: McGraw Hill.

Penn, H (2012) Childcare Markets: Do They Work?, in Lloyd, E and Penn, H (eds) *Childcare Markets: Can They Deliver an Equitable Service?* Bristol: Policy Press.

Randall, V (2000) *The Politics of Child Daycare in Britain*. Oxford: Oxford University Press.

Rousseau, J (1979) *Emile: Or on Education*. (A Bloom, Trans.). New York, NY: Basic Books (Original work published in 1762).

States of Jersey (2008) The Official Website for Public Services and Information Online, Government and Administration. [online] Available at: www.gov.je/Government/Pages/default.aspx (accessed 17 April 2014).

Tomlinson, P (2013) *Early Years Policy and Practice: A Critical Alliance*. Northwich: Critical Publishing.

Wincott, D (2005) Devolution, Social Democracy and Policy Diversity in Britain: The Case of Childcare and Early Years Policies. Institute for Public Policy Research (North). [online] Available at: http://www.ippr.org/assets/media/uploadedFiles/ipprnorth/events/2004/sem1-paper%20 on%20childcare.pdf (accessed 25 November 2014).

3 Russia: Golden Key Schools

COLETTE MURPHY AND NOIRIN HAYES

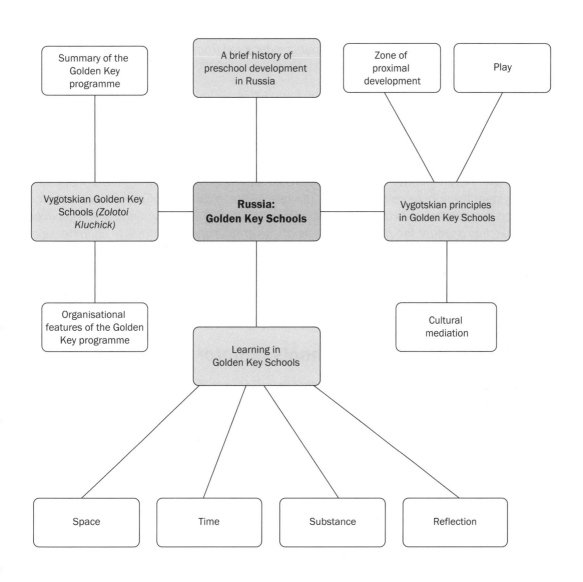

A brief history of preschool development in Russia

The government reforms of 1861 in Russia marked the beginning of public preschool education and recognition of its importance in liberating and developing the individual (Taratukhina et al, 2006). However, it was the founding in 1871 of the first Fröbel Society at St Petersburgh that led to the establishment of training for women to provide education for preschool children. The society also provided a site for discussion on theory and practice of child psychology and preschool education.

By the beginning of the twentieth century there was a variety of different preschool services throughout Russia with different educational ambitions and underlying principles. Following the 1917 revolution all preschools came under the direction of the People's Commissariat of Education. Underpinning the development of preschool education were principles of equality for women, their participation in the labour market and '*the collectivization of everything including children...The idea of collective public education from the youngest age was a central tenet of Soviet education theory*' (Taratukhina et al, 2006, pp 3–4).

Despite Vygotsky's work being carried out during this period, his ideas did not influence Soviet education policy, which focused more on collective labour. Indeed, Vygotsky's works were suppressed until after Stalin's death in 1953. Although his followers kept his work in the field of child and educational psychology to the fore of research internationally, it is only since *Perestroika* in the early 1990s that Vygotsky's theories have significantly informed research and development in Russia. *Perestroika* saw movement away from a unitary education system towards more diversity. By the late 1990s a network of preschools provided education '*oriented towards the needs of society and offering a variety of education services which take into account the particular needs of age groups and individuals in child development*' (Taratukhina et al, 2006, p 6). Preschools are now free to select their own curricular programme from a range of options, all of which recognise the importance of individual-social development and teacher–child interactions and stress the cultural–historical and active approach central to Vygotsky's educational ideas. In this chapter we describe a preschool following one such preschool curriculum – The Golden Key.

Vygotskian Golden Key Schools (*Zolotoi Kluchick*)

Elena Kravtsova (Lev Vygotsky's granddaughter), Gennadi Kravtsov and their colleagues at the Vygotsky Institute of the Russian State University for the Humanities developed the Golden Key programme. More than 30 Golden Key Schools have been established since 1989, each following the principles of Vygotsky and cultural–historical psychology.

Summary of the Golden Key programme

The Golden Key programme was developed from consideration of the work of several programmes and scholars including: Swedish kindergartens, the English nurturing system, Rudolf Steiner's anthroposophy and Waldorf pedagogy, in combination with the seminal work on child development and learning carried out by Vygotsky, his co-workers and followers.

The founders of the Golden Key Schools were themselves students of actual followers of Vygotsky; Elena Kravtsova's teacher was A V Zaporozhets and Gennadi Kravtsov was a student of Daniil El'konin. Golden Key teachers undergo an immersion programme as part of their training. They live, work, study and contribute to life in the community where the school is based. They study psychology, which in Russia embraces education and drama. Pedagogy draws directly on these areas and Golden Key teachers are highly skilled in the creative arts, such as music, drama and role-play, which are vital to the delivery of their curriculum.

The main principles of Golden Key Schools are to be found in the words 'culture' and 'history'. People are dualistic beings, belonging both to the worlds of nature and culture and they possess both a basic natural psyche and cultural higher psychological functions. Vygotsky's main criticism of traditional child psychology was that it did not embrace the history of a child's cultural development. He proposed a more holistic theory of development that combined cognitive, social, physical, emotional and cultural influences.

Critical questions

»   *Can this approach only work where children have shared historical and cultural backgrounds?*

»   *How in your experience do practitioners know about the culture and history of children in their setting?*

CASE STUDY

A Golden Key School in Belaya Kalitva

This case study describes the application of Vygotskian cultural–historical principles in one particular Golden Key School in Belaya Kalitva in the Rostov region of Southern Russia, close to the border with Ukraine. The findings are drawn from first-hand observation during a recent 'immersion' summer school for international scholars.

The disintegration of the Soviet Union and consequent collapse of national planning, in favour of the introduction of markets for industrial goods, caused significant shock waves in many small industrial cities such as Belaya Kalitva (Population: 43,651 – 2010 All-Russian Population Census – Vol 1: Federal State Statistics Service, 2011) as they made the transition to a market economy. The bedrock industry for Belaya Kalitva was aluminium production. As guaranteed orders from the old Soviet system contracted, so did production. The resulting unemployment had catastrophic social consequences, including high rates of alcoholism. Belaya Kalitva had survived on the industrial wages of employees of the aluminium factory, and taxes levied by local government paid for services such as health and education. During transition to a market economy there was a collective sense of loss as citizens saw Soviet structures being dismantled. The state could no longer be relied on to provide work, accommodation, health and education. It was against this cultural–historical backdrop that the first Golden Key School in the Rostov region was established.

Organisational features of the Golden Key programme

The fundamental organisational features of the Golden Key programme are based around five principles.

1. *Mixed-age as well as single-age group teaching,* which allows older children to reflect their own learning by helping younger children who, in turn, benefit from learning from people closer to their own age and stage.

2. *Family principles, including parental involvement,* underlie school organisation. Schools take children aged three to ten years.

3. *Lessons are centred on 'events'* that are highly meaningful to children and engage their emotions. Consequently, each lesson follows a 'plot' relating directly to the event. The 'event' we witnessed was the arrival of a letter delivered directly to the classroom. This letter was from a wolf, desperately seeking help from the children to find his fairy tale – he had jumped out of the book and could not remember to which tale he belonged. A series of activities was based around finding 'clues' from which, eventually, the children could determine the correct tale for the wolf. Such activities, some of which were carried out in mixed-age groups involving older children helping younger ones, and other age-specific activities based on mathematics, science, verbal and spatial reasoning, geography, comprehension, history, drama etc were enacted over the period of a week. Children were fully engaged and many of the skills they demonstrated in enacting the traditional curricular requirements, such as mental arithmetic, compositional writing and logical reasoning, were considered by the authors to be very advanced for the children's ages. They seemed to be working 'a head taller than themselves' (Vygotsky, 1978, p 102) in the quest to find the wolf's tale.

4. *Interaction and interdependence of education and development,* so that 'lessons' for younger children are not structured in the same way as those for older children. Learning takes place within the 'zone of proximal development', a construct attributed to Vygotsky's work (discussed in detail later in this chapter).

5. *Paired pedagogy,* in which some teaching is enacted by more than one teacher. Typically, one acts as a traditional 'teacher' while the second acts in an 'under' role by, for example, asking naïve questions which are answered easily by the children: sometimes this teacher has not been present earlier and asks children to explain and therefore reflect on their learning; other times the second teacher takes on the role of 'fool', acting silly and requiring multiple corrections of her/his poor attempts to keep up. One of the authors has carried out similar work using puppets, instead of adults, in the role of 'under' teacher (Murphy, 2009).

Critical question

»   *To what extent do these principles describe a child-led pedagogy?*

Vygotskian principles in Golden Key Schools

Three specific Vygotskian principles underlie much of learning and teaching in Golden Key Schools: the zone of proximal development, play and cultural mediation. Each will be considered theoretically and practically as applied in Golden Key Schools.

Zone of proximal development

There is currently much debate about what Vygotsky actually meant by the 'zone of proximal development' (ZPD). The simplistic definition of the ZPD found in many textbooks and other publications is of the 'gap' between what a child can achieve unaided and with help. For example, Gredler and Sheilds (2008) described Vygotsky's experiment, which showed that a group of eight-year-old children with the same 'actual' level of cognitive development were not all able to solve a new problem, given equal amounts of help. Despite scoring the same on an IQ test, one child solved the task with very little help, while others did not solve it even after several different interventions designed to support the learning. Vygotsky considered performance on summative tests as an indication of the child's past knowledge and argued *'instruction must be orientated towards the future, not the past'* (Vygotsky, 1934, 1962, p 104). He described the ZPD as maturing psychological functions that are required for understanding more abstract concepts. The conditions required to 'create' a ZPD to promote maturation of these functions are of prime importance to children's development of scientific concepts.

In the Golden Key Schools, ZPD creation to enhance children's learning is facilitated by mixed-age teaching, paired pedagogy and situating children's learning in contexts which are meaningful, interesting and which motivate them to learn. Essentially, creating a ZPD enables children to think and act 'higher' than they would otherwise.

Play

There is a vast amount of literature about play in the early years, much of it debating whether the focus should be on teaching academic skills or engaging young children in make-believe play as a developmental activity (Bodrova and Leong, 2007), and recently the focus has fallen more on the former. Bodrova and Leong (2007) suggest there is a false dichotomy between play and academic skills when considered from a Vygotskian perspective. Indeed, Vygotsky maintained that creating an imaginary situation in play is a means by which a child can develop abstract thought. He considered play as a precursor to academic learning in two ways (Murphy, 2012; see Figure 3.1).

The best kind of play to develop abstract thought is where children use unstructured and multifunctional props, as opposed to those that are realistic. The former type of props strongly promotes language development to describe their use; for example, a cardboard box may serve first as a shop, then as a school, then as home. Vygotsky said that this repeated naming and renaming in play helps children to master the symbolic nature of words, which leads to realisation of the relationship between words and objects, and then of knowledge and the way knowledge operates.

PLAY

- Helps children develop the ability to self-regulate their physical, social and cognitive behaviours by the use of 'rules' in their games.

- Places restraints on a child's actions and forces them to practise self-regulation (NB: this only happens when children are able to create a joint imaginary situation, take on roles of pretending characters and act these out using imaginary props, languages and symbolic gestures).

- Helps children develop abstract thinking via the use of objects, eg, toys, props, clothes, in make-believe play. Such use of objects for pretend, rather than real-life purposes, serves as a bridge between sensory-motor manipulation of objects and fully developed logical thinking, when the child can manipulate ideas in their heads.

- Using various props to separate the 'meaning' of the object from the object itself, eg, to drive a block on a carpet as if it were a truck (gives the block 'truckness') acts as a precursor to abstract thought.

Figure 3.1 *Ways that imaginative play is a precursor to academic learning (adapted from Murphy, 2012).*

Vygotsky promoted the notion that play as learning should lead development, as opposed to the more accepted notion of development leading learning or play. Learning that takes place within children's play is discussed by Nikolai Veresov (2005), who uses Vygotsky's example of a child playing with a stick by using it as a horse. The child learns about the object (stick) and its objective physical properties but will also decide whether such properties allow or prevent the stick from becoming a horse. If the object does not suit the play task, the child will stop playing with it. Veresov posits that learning in play is movement from the field of *sense* to the field of *meaning*; that '*sense finds a suitable object, that is, sense objectifies itself*' (p 13).

Vygotsky theorists point towards empowering children through play. For example, when modelling a situation in play involving, say, an imaginary parent or teacher or grocer or doctor, the child becomes in Vygotsky's terms '*a head taller*' (Vygotsky, 1978). Vygotsky himself suggested that play creates a ZPD of the child:

> *This strict subordination to rules [during play] is quite impossible in life, but in play it becomes possible: thus, play creates a zone of proximal development of the child. In play a child always behaves beyond his average age, above his daily behavior; in play it is as though he were a head taller than himself.*

(p 102)

In Golden Key Schools, teachers promote role-play and imaginary play in learning for children throughout the early years and primary school to further the development of abstract, conceptual thought. There is less focus on individual play with objects and more on collective play; Vygotsky's perspective on play connected it to the socio-cultural context in which a child is raised. He suggested that adults and older children should also be involved to model both roles and the use of props for the younger ones.

Much research and theoretical development on play has been conducted at the Vygotsky Institute at the Russian State University for the Humanities in Moscow. They have taken Vygotsky's ideas about the importance of play and constructed a sophisticated understanding of how it supports children's learning and development. These types of activities (in order of appearance) include:

- *object manipulation* – simple manipulation of objects;

- *director's play* – a child's individual play with objects creating imaginary situations;

- *image play* – a child exploring different roles by creating different images – eg, dressing up;

- *subject plot role play* – children playing with each other with shared plots, where they are the subject of the play; and

- *games with rules* – playing games with rules that include some form of an imaginary situation.

Critical questions

» *Thinking of imaginary play activities in different early years settings you know, can you find examples to fit all of the above categories?*

» *Is this true of all types of settings across the sector?*

Vygotsky (1933, 1967) explained the importance of 'imaginary situations' in play:

> *From the point of view of development, the fact of creating an imaginary situation can be regarded as a means of developing abstract thought. I think that the corresponding development of rules leads to actions on the basis of which the division between work and play becomes possible, a division encountered as a fundamental fact at school age.*
>
> (p 28)

A child's understanding of, and ability to distinguish effectively between, the imaginary situation and the real context are important in the development of abstract thought. Vygotsky ends his discussion by arguing how this develops into an understanding of external reality and thought.

> *At school age play does not die away, but permeates the attitude toward reality. It has its own inner continuation in school instruction and work (compulsory activity based on rules). All examinations of the essence of play have shown that in play a new relationship is created between the semantic and the visible – that is, between situations in thought and real situations.*
>
> (p 29)

During a two-week-long demonstration of pedagogy at Golden Key School in Belaya Kalitva, the teachers were observed creating an imaginary context for the children to engage with by giving them an encoded letter from a wolf (see the earlier description in 'Organisational features of the Golden Key programme'). Within the Golden Key curriculum and pedagogy, adults can and should have an important role in promoting play that supports development and a significant portion of the school day at a Golden Key School is centred on preparation for an *event* or *happening*. This includes an integrated approach to all areas of the curriculum around the theme or story of the event, which is, in some ways, similar to a core curriculum approach. The children engaged in activities throughout the week culminating in an event on the last day – the performance of the wolf's story with music, dance, costumes and dialogue. The event-centred curriculum brings us to a third important aspect of development, cultural mediation.

Cultural mediation

While it is commonly observed that children learn from adults and other children, it is less obvious how this happens. Vygotsky suggested that the child appropriates cultural tools and ways to use them, interacting with the environment via the mediation of cultural agents. The child is the subject, not the object of learning. Piaget, on the other hand, argued that the child's learning represented biological adaptation to the environment, a far more passive role.

The main cultural tool, according to Vygotsky, is language, a sign system. Vygotsky noted the importance of cultural mediation of these sign systems in humans, which does not occur in animals. For instance, in the everyday activity of eating, animals of a particular species all eat in the same way, whereas in humans, how someone eats strongly reflects the culture in which they were raised and there are many, many different ways in which humans consume food. Vygotsky argued that cultural mediation is just as important in consideration of how, and indeed what, children learn.

It must be remembered that the 'mediator', such as language, carries *meaning and sense* as well as functioning as a tool, and must therefore be *interpreted* by the child (Zinchenko, 2007). Therefore, the child contributes to the culture, and continues this contribution in many ways throughout his or her life. The child's role in learning and development is perceived as much more active and agentic with a Vygotskian interpretation of how learning occurs through interaction with their environment than if we use the Piagetian model based on children's adaptation to the environment. Piaget's model leaves little room for the child to alter the environment as a consequence of their learning. The use of language, ZPD and imaginary play supports a child's mediation with the culture as they develop in the context of their family, school, local culture and global environment.

The Golden Key curriculum and pedagogy support this mediation through the deliberate creation of opportunities for children to actively engage with culturally significant events. Children may explore fairy tales, help an imaginary hero return home from another country, participate in national celebrations, or perform traditional dances. The juxtaposition of the real and imaginary helps children understand the world they live in and as they reach school age develop academic skills and knowledge. The success of the Golden Key Schools provides support for the value of the cultural–historical perspective of development and learning. For example, the school we visited in Belaya Kalitva recorded high rates of college attendance and a zero rate of alcoholism among its graduates, which was significant in a town that suffered extremely high rates of alcoholism, especially among young people.

Critical question

» *The examples above describe events centred on traditional stories. Do you think this would work in your context? Would it work with topics taken from popular culture, such as superheroes, celebrities or TV characters?*

Learning in Golden Key Schools

Vygotsky proposed a 'super-concept' framework that defines all human activity within the environment. There are four major concepts in this framework (Kravtsova, 2010), which underlie all teaching in Golden Key Schools. Children are oriented in the world via these four super-concepts, which, the Golden Key teachers explain, is necessary for children who have not been born into a large, extended, family-based community structure in which they 'see' their lives planned ahead of them via siblings, cousins, parents, aunts, uncles, grandparents, etc. Many children from Belaya Kalitva are from small families who moved to the city after the break-up of the Soviet Union and are hence disconnected from extended family and community. Psychologically this can lead to disorientation at a young age, and teachers strive to re-orient children in the world through their early schooling. The super-concepts are:

- *space* – all human activity takes place within a certain space, or place;
- *time* – all human activity in the world occurs in a certain time;
- *substance* – all human activity uses substance, or materials; and
- *conscious reflection* – activity in humans differs from other animals because of the element of reflection on what to improve in the action or activity, and how this improvement could be made.

Space

When children start at the age of three, space is the first focus. They are 'oriented' first in a group space within the room, then in their own space within that group. They begin their exploration of space by working with the teachers to set up the room. Discussions begin about relative location. A teacher may ask questions about how to decorate the room – where a picture or map should be placed. They bring in artefacts from home, including photographs or small ornaments, which are placed on each child's table area, and thus link the school place with the home place. Older children then take the younger ones around the school and gradually introduce them to the whole school and all who work there, including the other teachers, catering and cleaning colleagues. Early work with maps includes showing how to find other rooms in the school. When children are totally familiarised with the school, they reflect this learning by inviting parents and relatives to the school and giving them a tour of the school and its community. The 'place' orientation continues as children develop by orienting themselves in the 'space' between home and school, then in the local area, etc. We observed in every classroom a set of large wall maps superimposed on each other so that children can orientate 'place' in all of their learning. For example, behind a map of the town was one of the province, behind this a map of Russia, then Europe and so on until the maps at the back were of the cosmos.

Teachers support children's ongoing exploration of space by creating imaginary journeys connected to the event at the core of the lesson; they may plan, for example, a journey to rescue a hero from another country. These multi-age imaginary expeditions provide many opportunities for children to engage in learning in a wide ZPD. Teachers provide contexts for older and younger children to explore life, Earth and physical science concepts. They set up imaginary interactions during the children's 'travel'. On their imaginary journey they may

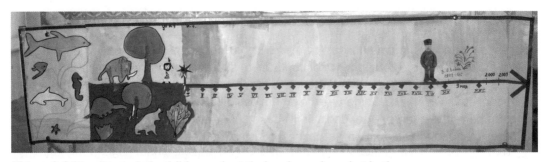

Figure 3.2 *Timeline to help children orient their science learning in time.*

look, for example, at which side of the rocks moss grows or where the Sun is – developing a connection with moss and the Sun. Older children discuss these connections with younger children. Children are introduced to, for example, the three states of matter by 'encountering' water as steam, water and ice or snow in their adventure. A study of plants in their rooms may expand to learning about plants found in different parts of the world. Children may talk about which plants grow only in the north or the south, in sunlight or shade, or soil characteristics, etc.

A fundamental assumption in this curriculum is that experiences with space, both local and distant, through imagination and story, combine to provide an orientation to the world that is important in the child's future generalisation of theory and understanding of relationships between elements of the natural world.

Time

Children are oriented similarly within the concept of time. Figure 3.2 shows a timeline that children constructed as a 'time-based' activity for their own classroom. Each classroom has a child-constructed timeline stretching across a wall. Timelines start with the beginning of life, and children can orient their learning in time using this. For instance, they can mark the times when dinosaurs roamed the Earth, the discoveries of fire, the wheel, the solar system, electricity, the Moon landings, historical events, family history, etc. They can use the timeline to visualise life spans of large trees, humans and elephants and to consider themselves in relation to older members of their family, ascendants and younger members.

During the study of time the school creates a 'time machine' and during their 'time travel' they become aware of great events and discoveries from the past. They realise there was a time before electricity was harnessed and explore a time with no cars, where horses and candles were used instead of cars and electric lights. The goal is to help children to experience, in imaginary play situations, life before these discoveries. The time machine also 'takes' children to the future – allowing them to use their spacecraft to travel to planets, solar systems and galaxies. Through imaginary travel, they investigate the cosmos and compare it to Earth. For example children may compare the pressure, temperature and length of day on Venus to that on Earth.

The placement of the present day in terms of their cultural–historical context is viewed as important to facilitate children's mediation with their world and in turn promote development. As with children's interaction with space, imaginary and real interaction with time by a multi-age group and with the support of teachers promotes development and foundational, both real and imaginary, encounters with scientific concepts.

Substance

In relation to the 'substance' concept, children use materials in different ways depending on their age. Early exploration of materials is important for language development. As children get older they focus on manipulating a wide variety of materials and theorising on these experiences to arrive at logical explanations of phenomena. Vygotsky maintained that children at the elementary level need to be encouraged in such learning activities, which are vital for later development of conceptual thought within concepts constructed by generations of historians, scientists, etc.

Reflection

The concept of reflection encompasses conscious awareness of the world and children's 'place' in it, as well as reflecting learning from older to younger children and vice versa. In addition, Vygotsky was interested in reflecting ideas, stories, etc, from the inside-out or back-to-front, and Golden Key teachers use reflection to test children's understanding by, for instance, inviting them to write a story, such as Cinderella, in which the heroine becomes the villain.

Critical question

» *Do you agree that a 'super-concept' framework would help to support children who are not embedded in an extended family or local community? How could a 'super-concept' framework be used to support planning in your context?*

Conclusion

These four themes support the experiences and development of the children through intentional play experiences, learning leading development in the ZPD and cultural mediation. The development of these four themes is for the group rather than for individual children at a certain age. Holzman (1997) discusses the four themes at the Golden Key Schools:

> It is important to emphasize that it is not the child's year (first, second, and so on) being referred to, but the multiage group's year, lest the above be understood as equivalent to or even similar to grade level. The organizing principle (the philosophical structure) of this alternative educational model is the ongoing development of the group as it creates itself as a group that is developing and changing. To me, this focus on the group is what – in Vygotskian fashion – allows for the 'good learning' that the Golden Key documents for all its children.

(p 90)

Critical reflections

Reflecting on our observations, we concluded that Golden Key Schools, classrooms, and classes are very different from the typical. Their teachers learn the value of imaginary experiences and fully implement the ZPD with 'learning leading development', combined with an understanding that development is also a process of cultural mediation, rather than primarily a biological process.

We felt what we observed validates many pedagogical approaches supported by research and opens the door to investigate interesting ways of thinking about providing science experiences for children from ages three to ten years old. These innovative and theoretically grounded approaches to create learning experiences in children's ZPD, to make use of imaginary experiences (play), and to help children connect with and learn from their culture and history, provide rich opportunities to bring new insights and ways of thinking about teaching and learning in a variety of contexts.

The theoretical influence of Vygotsky and his emphasis on the activity approach therefore continues to influence and now informs the training and education of preschool teachers so that, as Burlakova (2010, p 35) reflects, future teachers competent in developmental education will get fundamentally different psychological preparation that allows them to 'see' and to understand the role of activity in preschoolers' development.

Further reading

Gredler, M and Clayton Sheilds, C (2008) *Vygotsky's Legacy: A Foundation for Research and Practice.* New York: The Guildford Press.

Provides an overview of Vygotsky's work, extending beyond familiar topics like zone of proximal development, with useful examples of the major theoretical constructs in action.

Holzman, L (1997) *Schools for Growth: Radical Alternatives to Current Educational Models.* Mahwah, NJ: Lawrence Erlbaum Associates, Inc.

Includes a chapter on Golden Key Schools as part of a wider exploration of 'developmental learning' inspired by Vygotsky and Wittgenstein.

Vygotsky, L S (1933/1967). Play and Its Role in Mental Development. *Soviet Psychology,* 5(3): 6–18. Translated by Catherine Mulholland. [online] Available at: www.marxists.org/archive/vygotsky/works/1933/play.htm (accessed June 2014).

Vygotsky's classic article on play (originally a speech) now available online.

References

Bodrova, E and Leong, D (2007) Playing for Academic Skills, in *Rediscovering Vygotsky: The Eduring Impact of a Russian Psychologist.* Special edition of *Children in Europe*: 10–11.

Burlakova, I A (2010) New Requirements to Preschool Curriculum as a Guideline for Teachers Preparation. *Psychological Science and Education*, 3: 32–7.

Gredler, M and Clayton Sheilds, C (2008) *Vygotsky's Legacy: A Foundation for Research and Practice*. New York: The Guildford Press.

Holzman, L (1997) *Schools for Growth: Radical Alternatives to Current Educational Models*. Mahwah, NJ: Lawrence Erlbaum Associates, Inc.

Kravtsova, E E (2010) The Cultural–Historical Foundations of the Zone of Proximal Development. *Journal of Russian and East European Psychology*, 47(6): 9–24.

Murphy, C (2009) Vygotsky and Primary Science. Presentation given at the Vygotsky Summer School, Belaya Kalitva, Russia.

Murphy, C (2012) Vygotsky and Primary Science, in Fraser, B J, Tobin K G and McRobbie, C J (eds) *Second International Handbook of Science Education*. Dordrecht, Netherlands: Springer, 177–87.

Taratukhina, M S, Polyakova, M N, Berezina, T Q, Notkina, N A, Sheraizina, R M and Borovkov, M I (2006) Early Childhood Care and Education in the Russian Federation. Background Paper prepared for the Education for all Global Monitoring Report 2007. Strong Foundations: Early Childhood Care and Education. UNESCO.

Veresov, N (2005) Zone of Proximal Development (ZPD): The Hidden Dimension?, in Ostern, A-L and Heilä-Ylikallio, R (eds) *Language as Culture – Tensions in Time and Space*. Vasa: ABO Akademi, 1: 13–30.

Vygotsky, L S (1933/1967) Play and Its Role in Mental Development. *Soviet Psychology*, 5(3): 6–18. Translated by Catherine Mulholland. [online] Available at: http://www.marxists.org/archive/vygotsky/works/1933/play.htm (accessed June 2014).

Vygotsky, L S (1934, 1962) *Thought and Language*. Cambridge, MA: MIT Press.

Vygotsky, L S (1978) *Mind in Society: The Development of Higher Psychological Processes*. Cambridge, MA: Harvard University Press.

Zinchenko, V P (2007) Thought and Word: The Approaches of L S Vygotsky and G G Shpet, in H Daniels, M. Cole, and J V Wertsch (eds) *The Cambridge companion to Vygotsky*. NY: Cambridge University Press, pp. 212–45.

4 The complex construction of professionalism in ECEC services in Italy

FEDERICA CARUSO AND PAOLO SORZIO

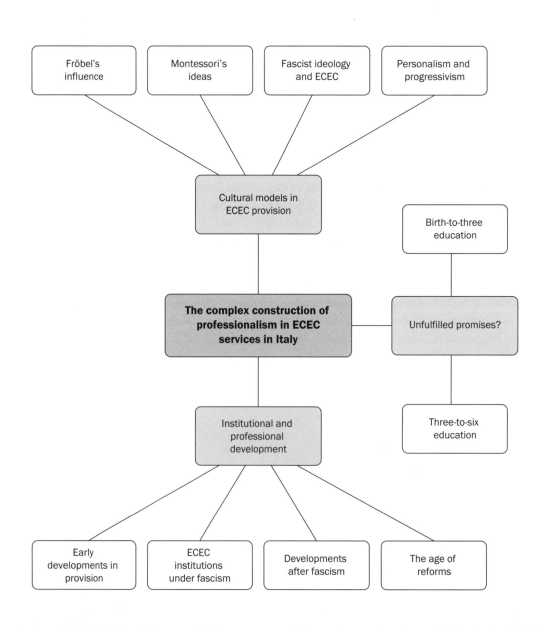

Introduction

This chapter analyses early childhood education and care (ECEC) provision in Italy according to cultural, institutional and professional areas of development. The history of ECEC in Italy can be conceptualised as the interplay between different cultural models and policies, which at times has reached a balance and produced innovative change. Over the years, geographical differences have persisted: the metropolitan areas of Northern and Central Italy had developed a system of ECEC even before Unification (1861). In Southern Italy, public structures for early childhood services were less developed and later implementation has been difficult and fragmented. Another discontinuity in ECEC provision relates to children's age. In Italy responsibility for ECEC from birth to three-year-olds falls to the Regions, whereas provision for three- to six-year-olds forms part of the national system of schooling. Some municipalities are notable exceptions and have developed and financially supported integrated provision as a public welfare service for children and families.

The chapter is organised around four main themes, characterising different aspects of professionalism in ECEC in Italy.

1. Different cultural models relevant to ECEC practice.

2. Structures of institutional practices in ECEC during different historical periods.

3. Promises of an integrated and widespread system of ECEC throughout the country.

4. Problematic and unfulfilled aspects of ECEC provision.

Cultural models in ECEC provision

Fröbel's influence

Following Italy's Unification (1861), Fröbel's writings were the main source of inspiration for establishing kindergartens. Two divergent interpretations predominated: the first emphasised the philosophical aspects of Fröbel's thinking, the role of early childhood education and care in maintaining original harmony between nature and the idealised child. Leading figures Rosa and Carolina Agazzi established a kindergarten in Mompiano (Lombardy) in 1895, which inspired the traditional approach to ECEC; working in nurseries and in kindergartens was considered a gender-specific activity, focused on the emotional and behavioural aspects of children's development. Children's personality was defined in terms of innateness, spontaneity and simplicity, and the cognitive and social aspects of children's minds overlooked. The role of the teacher was limited to preservation of continuity between family and community, and nurturing children's innate dispositions. Every activity, whether language learning or natural observation, should be approached consistently as play, since play is regarded as the 'natural' dimension of children's mental conception (Agazzi, 1898). Furthermore, the teacher should establish a code of behaviour based on obedience to adults and restore moral order when children's bad behaviour disturbs the peaceful community. According to this conception of ECEC professionalism, teachers required only limited pre-service education.

The second interpretation of Fröbel's writings mainly overlooked philosophical aspects and focused more on educational method, promoting children's active engagement through structured toys (the 'gifts'). Teachers' professional competencies were promoted through initial and in-service education. Education was perceived as an opportunity to support child development through participating in social life; municipality-led kindergartens started in Venice in 1896 and in Reggio Emilia in 1911 (the kernel of the more recent Reggio system).

Montessori's ideas

Maria Montessori developed an original approach to ECEC through direct practice in the newly established 'Children's House' in Rome. She understood children's development as movement from the immediacy of their needs and impulses to subsequent structured personality and intelligence, through their active engagement in constant activity. Teachers have a mediating role in children's development through designing stimulating environments with appropriate resources. On an emotional level, teachers should avoid authoritarian attitudes towards children's 'efforts'. Cognitively, they should support children's reflections on experience, connections between physical actions and their imagination and planning skills (Montessori, 1913). In 1934 the 'Children's House' was banned by fascists; Montessori emigrated and her model is still more appreciated abroad than in Italy.

Fascist ideology and ECEC

A third educational model operated in Italy during fascism (1922–43). As a totalitarian state, fascism did not tolerate differences in values and cultural perspectives between the state and individual consciousness; the ECEC system therefore formed an integral part of state control over infancy and women. Progressive experiences were suppressed; teachers were forced to swear fidelity to the regime and transmit values of strength and discipline to male children, and devotion to female ones.

In 1923 a first school reform (signed by the philosopher Giovanni Gentile) stated that:

> *the maternal schools [as the kindergarten were renamed] will care, protect and facilitate children's natural development and – at the same time – will impress habits of joyful and conscious obedience and discipline, in his [emphasis on male gender in original text] soul and life.*

The programme made an explicit reference to political education in schools:

> *Considered in its operating concretisation, political education is, in its essence, a process of incorporation of the child's personality, from the short-sighted family groups to the more encompassing economic and political national groups and into the state that epitomises and unifies them all. This long and subtle process starts at the Maternal school, when the teacher is required to elicit and strengthen the feelings which will constitute the vital core of the political faith of the new citizen.*

The teachers were required to prepare *the new generations to act according to the values and ideals expressed by the fascist revolution*. As a consequence, teachers' professionalism was reduced to transmission of the regime's values and children's indoctrination. Educational pluralism and freedom of speech were suppressed.

Critical question

» *Consider your own beliefs about teaching. How would you respond to being told by the government to teach in a way that contradicts your beliefs?*

Personalism and progressivism

After the establishment of Republican democracy in Italy (1945 onward), two main approaches emerged: 'personalism' and progressive theory. Personalism held a very conservative view of ECEC, while the progressive approach promoted the introduction of new psychological and educational theories (Dewey, Piaget, Freud) into ECEC public discourse, although mainly localised in some municipalities. The hegemonic pedagogical theory for three- to six-year-olds was heavily shaped by personalism, which emphasises each person's 'uniqueness'. This perspective is in sharp contrast with individualism, since it stresses natural human tendencies towards virtues. Accordingly, teachers were expected to maintain connections between children and their communities and act sensibly, by matching children's naiveté. Teachers were indoctrinated into this perspective through professional journals and in-service education, led by national teacher associations; emergent theories in child psychology were not considered useful because they were associated with a positivistic stance and limited views of children's natural intuition of what is good.

In contrast, progressive education asserts that children need specifically designed environments to develop their social and cognitive attitudes. Therefore, ECEC is considered a fully educational space to promote children's social and personal identity, *'giving children the opportunity to develop an encompassing cultural and social view and promoting the development of every dimension of their identity'* (Ciari, 1972, p 219). Furthermore, ECEC offers an opportunity to compensate for differences in cultural access and prepare children for the cognitive requirements of later stages of schooling. Educators and teachers should become fully professionalised, since they must recognise children's initial knowledge, design stimulating activities to promote their learning and document activities. Many fruitful progressive ideas entered public discourse on ECEC during the 1970s. Through conferences and journals, they stimulated changes in other ECEC sectors in Italy, and eventually inspired the most innovative components of the reform documents in the National Frameworks of 1991 and 2012 (see below).

Critical question

» *How should teacher professionalism change in relation to the principles of progressive education?*

Institutional and professional development

Early developments in provision

In nineteenth and early twentieth centuries, working in ECEC services was very hard: two educators looked after about 100 children, for nine to ten hours a day and wages were very low. Marriage led to dismissal since the profession required unexhausted maternal devotion. Socialist organisations strove for educators' rights, good working conditions and higher wages. This active engagement for early childhood conditions and education led to diffusion of ECEC activities, especially in towns. According to Catarsi (1994), in 1907/08 there were 3576 nurseries and kindergartens in Italy, complemented by 1391 wards where poor children were supervised and fed. Services provided for 378,463 children with 7392 educators, only one third of whom had initial training. From 1910 to 1920 the number of ECEC institutions increased by 40 per cent and by 1920 there were 12,230 educators and teachers (Genovesi, 2000). In 1920, left-wing parties proposed the creation of at least one nursery and one kindergarten in each municipality. However, this progressive period was threatened by fascist violence, which led to Mussolini seizing power in 1922.

ECEC institutions under fascism

The main aim of ECEC during fascism was establishing discipline, obedience and faith in the fascist state from a young age.

CASE STUDY

Opera Nazionale Maternità e Infanzia

Fascism also developed a policy for mothers and early childhood (birth–three years) by establishing the *Opera Nazionale Maternità e Infanzia* (ONMI: National Organization for Maternity and Infancy) in 1925 (Act n. 2277, 10 December 1925). This institution was aimed at supervising every state and private initiative for the health, protection and safety of mothers and children, by starting a campaign for vaccination and nutrition. The explicit goal of the ONMI policy was to 'improve the Italian race':

> *to guarantee the woman, in her supreme function of maternity, any support adapted to the solemnity of her act of assuring the future of the species; and [to guarantee] the best assistance in promoting the healthy and strong growth of offspring, who, in turn, will constitute the basis of the country's youth as well as the breeding ground of pure and firm souls in defending and elevating the country.*

The ONMI policies were instrumental in maintaining the totalitarian state, since they promoted the identification of maternity with the country's fertility. They penetrated the sphere of intimacy avoiding activities that promoted self-confidence, autonomy and individual rights. Personal development and family initiatives were incorporated into general state ideology to suppress any space for dissent. Many of the leading figures of ONMI policies were also inspirers of racist legislation against Jews and other minorities from 1935 to 1938.

A capillary system of educational institutions was also created, in order to permeate every realm of life with the 'spirit' of fascism. Children from three years of age were forced to participate in out-of-school organisations that promoted fascist values, such as acceptance of hierarchy, the foundational myth of war, disdain for enemies, natural distinction between males and females, and the myth of race purity. A national system of initial education for teachers was established throughout Italy. Typically, two-year post-compulsory education was required to become a preschool teacher as well as active involvement in fascist organisations.

Critical question

» Both ONMI policies and Fröbel's writings value the role of women, but how does this differ between the two ideologies?

Developments after fascism

After the fall of fascism (1943–45) and the establishment of parliamentary democracy in Italy (from 1945 onwards), important reforms were enacted to promote the preschool system and teachers' professionalism. The *National Programme for the Maternal Schools* in 1958 formulated objectives for the education of three- to six-year-olds as '*the creation of relationships and continuity with the educational process already established in families*' (D P R n. 584, 1958, p 1); schooling from age three to six was therefore considered as support for families with children's education. The national government established a limited number of state-led schools and promoted a private system of Catholic-led maternal schools to support families in educating children according to their values. Families were considered static and homogeneous social institutions, although this was more a vision than reality, since Italy was undergoing a complex period of industrialisation, change of mentality and social mobility (Ginsborg, 2003).

Teachers needed either a three-year vocational certificate of education (usually at the age of 16) or an Italian certificate of secondary school education (at the age of 18) to teach both in maternal and in primary schools. They were recruited in state-led schools after public examination and in the private-led ones on the basis of a degree and acceptance of Catholic values. Along with state and private Catholic-led schools, some progressive municipalities set up local public schools and developed their own ECEC culture and documents, leading to more innovative educational initiatives and structures. In municipality-led ECEC systems, especially in central Italy, a strongly child-centred approach was implemented and as a consequence children's competencies and rights were recognised as the building blocks of the educational activities.

The most well-known initiative is the Reggio Emilia model. Loris Malaguzzi and his collaborators worked out an innovative system based on two important assumptions.

1. The centrality of children's competencies and creativity as the pivotal component of their development (constructivism).

2. The role of stimulating environments in supporting children's experience and learning.

Accordingly, the ECEC system was considered unitary from birth to six years of age, supporting continuity of children's development and consistency of educational methodology. Consequently, pre-service and in-service teacher education became crucial to develop Reggio Emilia pedagogy (Edwards, Gandini and Forman, 1998) and both nursery educators and teachers in preschools became professionalised, designing new environments that supported children's participation in education. Children contributed to the life of the schools by proposing activities, devising resources and realising artefacts, with the support of two innovative educational roles: the 'pedagogist' and the 'atelierist'. The 'pedagogist' is a co-ordinator teacher, whose role is the promotion of the quality of the educational provision through in-service teacher education and action-research. The 'atelierist' is an artist-in-residence in the school who supports the development of children's ideas in symbolic activities, such as dramatic plays and paintings.

The age of reforms

The late 1960s and the 1970s represented a period of innovation in ECEC, although birth-to-three educational provision was organised at regional level and three-to-six provision was part of the wider system of schooling.

Birth-to-three education

The National Act (1044/1971) established a new conception of birth-to-three education, by asserting the supportive role of nurseries for working women and their families. Although the text of the Act 1044/1971 did not explicitly mention the educational relevance of nurseries for children's development, it stressed the need for widespread systems of public educational services and the regions were assigned responsibility for the constitution of at least 3800 nurseries throughout Italy.

In the more cohesive regions, constitutive mandates for the establishment of nurseries explicitly recognised child-centred education; nursery schools were organised around children's opportunities to move and act creatively and teachers' professionalism was promoted with in-service programmes. Despite this, the regions still differ greatly both in the extent and quality of their provision.

Three-to-six education

The National Framework n. 647/1969 explicitly developed initiatives to overcome uneven diffusion of three-to-six-year education provision in Italian regions by organising a national system of free, state-led maternal schools. The number of teachers increased by 1240 per cent from 1968–69 to 1980–81 (Genovesi, 2000). As before, maternal school objectives are related more to childcare and family support than to promotion of children's competencies. Since teachers' professionalism is based on a supposed gendered personal attitude of care and sensitivity, there is little attention to professional knowledge in designing educational activities to promote children's development; a certificate of secondary school education was therefore still considered sufficient to teach in maternal schools.

The Act 463 in 1978 established a new organisation of education for three- to six-year-olds: schools opening for 10 hours a day; teachers' working schedule of 30 hours a week; two teachers team-teaching in each class; movement between classrooms, enabling children's participation in particular educational activities. From 1982 onwards, children with disabilities have been included in mainstream schools with the support of a specialised teacher and a ratio of one teacher for four children with disabilities; today specialised teachers still work to support colleagues with inclusion of children with special needs into mainstream classes. For over 20 years recruitment of teachers (three-to-six age range) was high; pupil:teacher ratios fell from 25.9:1 in 1969–70 to 10.8:1 in 1988–89 (Catarsi, 1994). Unfortunately, this ratio became higher again in the 2000s because of financial cuts and school restructuring.

In 1991 the more traditional and progressive models of three-to-six schooling achieved a balance in the newly established *Framework for Maternal Schools*, which introduced three important issues.

1.   For the first time in ECEC policies in Italy, it was explicitly maintained that three-to-six schooling is based on children's rights and needs to be educated, respected in their national, ethnic, linguistic, cultural and religious identity, as stated in the Italian Constitution.

2.   Schools are expected to promote integration of psychological, social and cultural dimensions of children's development. Learning is considered a process of acquisition of the cultural symbols to express oneself, to communicate and to explore the environment. Therefore, three-to-six schooling is a specialised public institution, where the main educational objective is to integrate children into wider society. Consequently, public three-to-six school provision should cover the whole country, teachers should develop new professional competencies, such as designing meaningful activities, team work and inclusion of more vulnerable children in mainstream school activities.

3.   The curriculum is organised in 'experiential fields', specific organisations of curricular activities to promote meaningful experience and learning in areas of children's interactions with the natural and social world (the self and the others; the body and movement; images, sounds and colours; words and discourses; knowledge of the world: objects, living kinds, numbers, forms). As maintained in the document: 'the teachers recognise and interpret the complexity of children's living experiences in their out-of-school practices, and therefore they are required to design school activities to promote children's self-awareness and understanding'. Usually, educational activities last from one week to three months, and directly refer to children's experiences (for example, their living space, seasons, animals). In participating in meaningful activities, children make use of cultural tools that promote their enculturation into specific symbolic languages and develop their identities, their knowledge of the world and a co-operative attitude.

In the official document, the educational sector for children ranging from three to six years of age is interchangeably called 'maternal school' or 'children's school', to stress the centrality of their ability to transform their earlier knowledge through well-designed meaningful experiences in school. Children's schools are considered part of the larger system of education, and teachers are therefore expected to work in teams, to design suitable activities in specific fields of experience, and to make curricular linkages with teachers of older children.

Because teachers' professionalism became more complex, a university Master's degree was proposed (and was eventually established with DM 26 May 1998) and a system of in-service education programmes developed, often conducted by teachers associations.

Unfulfilled promises?

Birth-to-three education

In her 1986 paper, Bondioli recognised the uncertain nature of nursery educators' professional culture, since it was suspended between replication of the maternal role and promotion of children's development, and highlighted the lack of public discussion about the professional identity of ECEC educators. In order to integrate nursery educators into a system of social promotion of child development and well-being, Catarsi (1988) called for a fully-fledged educational vision in birth-to-three education, in which nursery educators should be recognised as part of a 'wholly educating society' and as pivotal partners of families and school teachers in working out an educational project for all children. A group of educators, co-ordinated by Bertolini and Frabboni, both at the University of Bologna, recognised the different quality and distribution of birth-to-three education services in Italy, the sparse reality of innovative practices and educators' diverse working conditions and professional identity. They launched *A Proposal for the Constitution of a National Framework for Nursery Schools* (1998) to improve the quality of services and construct an early childhood culture. In this working paper, principal dimensions of professionalism in nursery education were recognised as:

- competencies in the design of settings, tools and educational activities to promote children's exploration of natural and social reality;

- competencies in recognising the complexity of children's development, in understanding children's intentions and responding to their actions; and

- competencies in reflective practice; thinking about their own educational activity to promote innovations and more advanced opportunities for children's learning. This reflective attitude requires expertise in observational methods, in educational design and in documentation.

The document also urged the establishment of university-level education for prospective nursery educators complemented with placement experience to promote competencies in educational design, observational methods and child psychology. Constant in-service education programmes are also encouraged to promote educators' personal and collaborative reflection on their professional practice and improvement of activities. Increased economical recognition (higher wages and job security) was also considered a crucial element in the qualification of educators' professionalism.

Unfortunately, this paper has never been translated into a fully-fledged policy paper and did not succeed, either as catalyst of public discussion on professionalism of birth-to-three educators, or as mediator in the development of widespread innovation in ECEC services. The institutional perspective moved from the need for an advanced culture among educators towards the increment of private services in ECEC, as a support for families, although with little educational vision. Private services compete with the public system of nurseries, offering reduced fees and greater flexibility in time schedules. Birth-to-three education remains loosely connected with the school system; its provision is highly variable in relation to the regional autonomies and educators' professionalism is also extremely variable. In many regions, educators do not have a university degree and in-service education is differentiated in contents and methods.

CASE STUDY

Professionalising birth-to-three provision in Emilia-Romagna

The Emilia-Romagna region can be considered an advanced model for the institutionalisation of birth-to-three provision. The Regional Act 1/10.01.2000 recognises all the children as subjects of individual, legislative, civic and social rights and operates to respect them as people. Consequently, nurseries are considered social and educational services, in the public interest (ie, not for profit), for all the children from three months to three years of age. The region establishes a policy framework oriented to children's well-being, promoting their right to be educated and respect for their identity. The newly introduced role of co-ordinator of each municipality system of nurseries is responsible for quality of educational service and in-service education programmes. Furthermore, the co-ordinator negotiates with policymakers to create networks with educational and recreational agencies in the wider community and guarantees continuity with preschool. Starting from 2015, in Emilia-Romagna a batchelor's university degree will be required to work as an educator in ECEC.

Critical question

> What differences might recognition of children's rights make to everyday practice in birth-to-three provision?

Three-to-six education

According to data presented by *CittadinanzAttiva* in 2008 to the Senate, there are more than 3000 certified nurseries in Italy, with about 130,000 placements and 23 per cent more requests for access, 59 per cent of nurseries are in northern Italy, 27 per cent in central regions and only 14 per cent in the south. The child:educator ratio varies, although usually it is 5:1 for infants and 7:1 for toddlers. Maximum numbers for childminders are seven children and micro-nurseries ten; playgroups accept eight children at maximum and are open only in the morning or afternoon. There are about 30,000 children's schools in Italy, uniformly distributed across the country, of which 13,485 are state-led and contain 43,233 classes for 1,030,364 children and 90,899 teachers (MIUR, 2013).

In 2012, the *General Framework for the Development of Competencies in Pre-primary and in the System of Initial Education* makes explicit that development of children's competencies forms the basis for lifelong learning. The system of 3- to 14-year-old pupils' education has been organised as comprehensive schooling to construct a longitudinal curriculum extending to lower secondary stages. The concept of 'fields of experience' is explicitly adopted as the template for later acquisitions in more traditional subjects.

Teachers in three-to-six provision are expected to collaborate with primary and secondary school colleagues to work out a curriculum that spans the school years and to document children's development. However, this approach has raised tensions between teachers at different grade levels, because they have developed very different cultural models about what the process of learning is. For pre-primary and primary teachers, the focus is more on child-centred activities; lower secondary teachers, however, believe the aim of schooling is getting students to learn subject contents. Furthermore, they claim that high-stakes standardised assessment tests put severe constraints on developing shared curriculum models for competencies. Finally, the economic crisis makes recruitment of young teachers with university degrees, specialised in the design and documentation of children-led educational activities, very difficult, as well as teachers' in-service education.

Conclusion

This chapter has described the history of the ECEC system in Italy and revealed considerable development over the last 40 years. However, two obstacles still hinder the development of professionalism in ECEC provision in Italy.

• Firstly, different cultural models of early childhood and educational services persist, because they are viewed as support for families. Expectations of professionals are limited to supporting children's emotions and looking after their spontaneous play. Little education is required for educators and teachers, since competencies in designing settings, tools and activities are not recognised. Recognition of the complexity of children's developmental processes and the importance of carefully designed educational activities requires, however, more advanced professionalism in educators and teachers.

• The second obstacle is the large differences in legislation concerning birth-to-three education among the regions. While there are areas in Italy well served by rich learning environments and well-prepared staff, other areas do not offer opportunities for children to attend educational activities in purpose-built settings, with the dynamic support of well-prepared educators. The most advanced areas promote well-qualified educators by requiring a university-level degree, as well as establishing manifold opportunities for in-service education.

Critical reflections

A main issue in ECEC is the different quality and diffusion of services in the Italian regions. A lively problem consists of the establishment of a system of circulation of practices and ideas for professionals.

Nurseries and children's schools are part of different institutional systems of ECEC: the former are under regional legislation and the latter are constitutive parts of the national system of schooling. Reasons to develop educational continuity between the two institutions should be carefully considered by policymakers and professionals as an opportunity to promote community growth and well-being for children and families.

In Italy, there is no shared theoretical framework to support educators' and teachers' professionalism. Although cultural debate between different perspectives is welcomed, it is also important to highlight the concepts and methods that are required, in order to structure initial education programmes and create a common knowledge among professionals.

Further reading

For reconstruction of ECEC in the Italian context, with insight into the most significant experiences:

Mantovani, S (2010) Italy, in P Oberhuemer, I Schreyer, M J Nueman (eds) *Professionals in Early Childhood Education and Care Systems. European Profiles and Perspectives*. Opladen & Farmington Hills: Barbara Budrich Publishers.

For in-depth analysis of the institutional problem of continuity in ECEC:

Lazzari, A and Balduzzi, L (2013) Bruno Ciari and 'Educational Continuity'. The Relationship from an Italian Perspective, in Moss, P (ed) *Early Childhood and Compulsory Education. Reconceptualising the Relationship*. London: Routledge.

The following offers an historical analysis of fascist policies for women and children:

De Grazia, V (1992) *How Fascism Ruled Women: Italy, 1920–1945*. Los Angeles: University of California Press.

For complete and updated normative references:

www.minori.it/en (accessed 5 December 2014)

References

Agazzi, R (1898) *Ordinamento dei giardini d'infanzia, secondo il sistema di Federico Fröbel* [Organization of Kindergartens, According to Fröbel's Pedagogy]. Torino: Paravia.

Bertolini, P and Frabboni, F (eds) (1998) *Proposta per un curricolo nazionale per la prima infanzia* [A Proposal for the National Framework for Nursery Schools], Infanzia, n. 7, marzo 1998, 1–64.

Bondioli, A (1986) *Un progetto di raccordo nido-materna in provincia di Pavia* [Analysis of a Linkage Between Nurseries and Preschools in Pavia], in V Cesareo and C Scurati (a cura di), *Infanzia e continuità educativa*. Milano: FrancoAngeli.

Catarsi, E (1988) *La continuità educativa tra l'asilo nido e la scuola materna* [Educational Continuity Between Nurseries and Preschools], in Infanzia, n. 5, 24–7.

Catarsi, E (1994) *L'asilo e la scuola dell'infanzia* [The Nurseries and the Preschools]. Firenze: La Nuova Italia.

Ciari, B (1972) *La grande disadattata* [The Great Maladjusted]. Roma: Editori Riuniti.

CittadinanzAttiva (2008) *Dossier: Asili Nido comunali in Italia.* [online] Available at: www.senato.it/documenti/ repository/commissioni/controllo_prezzi/documenti_acquisiti/Cittadinanzattiva_01_04_09_Asili_ nido_comunali.pdf [accessed 9 May 2014], [*Report on the Municipality-led System of Nursery Provision in Italy*].

D M 3 giugno (1991) *Orientamenti dell'attività educativa nelle scuole materne statali* [National Framework of Educational Activities in the State-led Maternal Schools].

D M 26 maggio (1998) *Criteri generali per la disciplina da parte delle università degli ordinamenti dei Corsi di laurea in scienze della formazione primaria e delle Scuole di specializzazione all'insegnamento secondario* [Standards for the University-led Schools for Primary and Secondary Teachers].

D P R n. 584, 11/06/1958, *Programmi didattici per le scuole materne* [National Programme for the Maternal Schools].

D P R n. 647, 10/09/1969, *Orientamenti dell'attività educativa nelle scuole materne statali* [National Framework of Educational Activities in the Maternal Schools].

Edwards, C, Gandini, L and Forman, G (1998) *The Hundred Languages of Children.* Norwood, MA: Ablex.

Genovesi, G (2000) *Storia della scuola in Italia dal Settecento a oggi* [History of the School System in Italy, since XVIII Century]. Bari: Laterza.

Ginsborg, P (2003) *Italy and Its Discontents. Family, Civil Society, State.* New York: Palgrave McMillan.

Legge n. 2277, 10 dicembre 1925, *Istituzione dell'Opera nazionale maternità e infanzia, per la protezione e l'assistenza della maternità e dell'infanzia* [Establishment of the National Organization for Maternity and Infancy, to Protect and Care for Maternity and Infancy].

Legge n. 1044, 6/12/1971, *Piano quinquennale per l'istituzione di asili-nido comunali con il concorso dello Stato* [A Five-year Master Plan to the Establishment of Municipality-led, State-supported Nurseries].

Legge n. 463, 9 agosto 1978, *Modifica dei criteri di determinazione degli organici e delle procedure per il conferimento degli incarichi del personale docente e non docente; misure per l'immissione in ruolo del personale precario nelle scuole materne, elementari, secondarie ed artistiche, nonche' nuove norme relative al reclutamento del personale docente ed educativo delle scuole di ogni ordine e grado* [Changes Introduced in the Standards to Define the Recruitment of Teachers and Staff in Preschools, Primary and Secondary Schools, Schools of Arts].

Legge Regionale Emilia Romagna n. 1, 10 gennaio 2000, *Norme in materia di servizi educativi per la prima infanzia* [Standards of the Early Childhood Education Services].

MIUR (2012) *Indicazioni Nazionali per il curricolo della scuola dell'infanzia e del primo ciclo di istruzion,* [General Framework for the Development of Competencies in Pre-primary and in the System of Initial Education].

MIUR (2013) Focus "Sedi, alunni, classi e dotazioni organiche del personale docente della scuola statale anno scolastico 2013/2014. [online] Available at: www.istruzione.it/allegati/avvio_anno_scolastico2013_2014_10.pdf [accessed 9 May 2014] [Dept of Education (2013) Venues, students, organisation and workforce of the State School System in 2013/2014].

Montessori, M (1913) *Il metodo della pedagogia scientifica applicato all'educazione infantile nelle 'Case dei bambini'*. Città di Castello: Lapi [Eng trans *Montessori's Method*, Chicago: Regnery].

Regio decreto n. 3106, 31/12/1923, *Grado preparatorio dell'istruzione elementare* [Preparatory Classes for Elementary Schools].

Part B
Gender and the workforce

5 Professionalisation processes and gender issues: the establishment of ECEC workforce in Sweden

SVEN PERSSON AND INGEGERD TALLBERG BROMAN

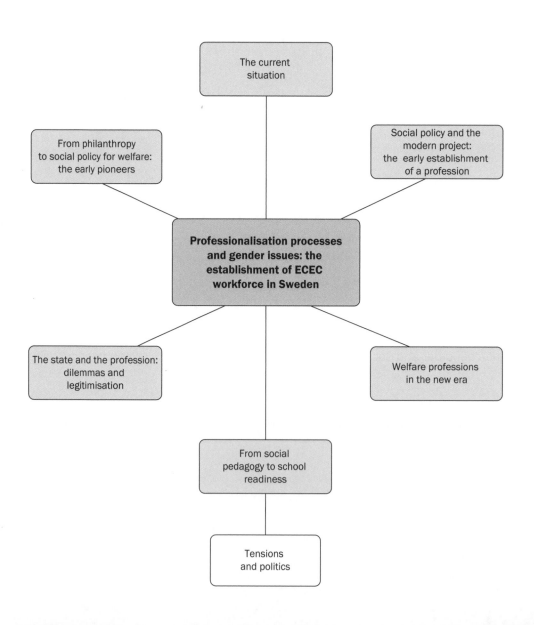

Introduction

In a historical perspective it is evident that Early Childhood Education and Care (ECEC) has made a crucial impact on Swedish society. The importance of the expansion of ECEC for the construction of the welfare state in Sweden is significant as it has influenced family and labour market policy, social equality and gender equality.

In this chapter we describe the expansion of ECEC institutions in Sweden, mainly using two concepts for analysing workforce development: professionalisation and gender. The common feature for the two concepts is the power dimension. The expansion of ECEC institutions and the development of a workforce in ECEC has struggled for legitimisation and cultural recognition in society. The struggle for professional legitimisation and the resistance it met are obviously related to power relations, gender issues and the acceptance of a female labour force.

The concept of profession is complex, and in this chapter we will use the term professionalisation *processes* to describe the strategies and pathways for legitimisation and recognition in society. Briefly, professionalisation processes include an endeavour by occupations to gain professional legitimisation in society, claiming that they have a specific and *unique competence* and knowledge about the professional object (in this case, children). Boundary markers (diplomas, language, symbols) are then used to distinguish the workforce knowledge from parents and caregivers. Traditionally, an academic diploma and university training have been a condition for professionals to claim that they have the scientific knowledge that is needed for the work. But professionalisation processes take place in several arenas. As shown in this chapter, informal networks, professional associations and unions are important arenas for defining professional knowledge and the working conditions that are needed. Professional legitimisation of the ECEC workforce is historically related to striving for recognition of ECEC institutions in society.

To understand the ECEC field we would emphasise the importance of a gender perspective. An expanded preschool of a general kind, which combines care and education, and which is offered to all families at a cost that everyone can afford, entails a thorough transformation of gender and power relations in a society. At the time when the field was initiated there was a patriarchal order and society was strictly divided according to class and gender, with few tasks or professions for women outside the home. In several countries, with Sweden as a clear example, the question of public involvement in childcare became a feminist issue with support from many quarters. The matter was pursued by feminists both outside and inside organisations. It was an issue chiefly for liberal and socialist feminists, not radical feminists (Randall, 1995). Bottom-up co-operation between feminist actions, and the support of the trade unions, chiefly LO, the Swedish Trade Union Confederation (although that was two-edged due to the support of 'femocrats ' in the political and administrative bureaucracy) were of crucial significance for the construction of the Swedish model. A central factor in the development of the whole 'equality project of preschool ' was the collaboration between lobby groups in politics, trade unions, active parents, and – not least of all – teachers working in preschool.

The form of family that is so dominant in the rest of Europe, 'male breadwinner – housewife' was also the model that applied to the family in Sweden up to the 1960s (Nauman, 2005). ECEC of present day dimensions had contributed in Sweden to a defamilialisation and an individualisation of man, woman and child alike. Women's dependence on the welfare state, taking the place of an earlier dependence on the husband/relatives, has been problematised using Scandinavian evidence (Hernes, 1987). Strategies and processes which we elucidate in this chapter are perceived as gendered and dependent on their gender and class context in society.

The current situation

Sweden has an integrated and comprehensive ECEC system for children under one leading ministry. The national curriculum for preschool, the Educational Act and the supporting material that is distributed by the National Agency have placed ECEC institutions in the discourse of education. While the national curriculum describes values, content, responsibilities and the overall task for preschool, it is up to the municipalities and the ECEC institutions to formulate and develop methods for practice. The decentralised system gives professional autonomy, that is freedom for preschool staff to develop educational practices that are based on local analysis, and for the municipalities to formulate strategies to develop the staff's knowledge and competence. The national curriculum describes goals to strive for in preschool and not the outcomes for the child.

There are three major types of ECEC institutions in Sweden: preschool, preschool class and educational care (formerly called family daycare). The vast majority of ECEC institutions in Sweden are preschools and preschool classes. Sweden differs from many other countries in its use of a transitional and non-compulsory preschool class for six-year-old children. Preschools are organised by the municipality or as independent preschools. The municipalities also organise *open preschools*, free to visit for parents on parental leave. Nearly 95,000 children attend independent preschools; this is equivalent to about 20 per cent of children in preschool (National Agency, 2014). All ECEC institutions, both municipal and independent, must follow the Education Act and the curriculum. The School Inspection examines the municipal preschools while independent preschools are reviewed by the municipality where they are located.

After a foundational phase for a model with a combination of care and education and a slow quantitative development, Swedish preschool was radically expanded in the last decades of the twentieth century. This is summed up in Table 5.1.

A high rate of Swedish children attend ECEC institutions. For children aged 0–3, 77 per cent attend ECEC institutions, 94 per cent of 4–5-year-olds and 94.7 per cent of 6-year-old children attend preschool classes (Statistics Sweden, 2013). Of 1-year-old children, 49 per cent attend ECEC institutions, but then we must bear in mind that parents often use parental leave until the child is one and a half years old.

There are two groups of staff in preschool in Sweden: preschool teachers and carers. They work closely together in teams. Approximately, 50 per cent of the staff are preschool teachers with a bachelor's degree. All educators (preschool teachers and carers) must have the

Table 5.1 Rate of children aged 1–6 attending preschool in 1975–2013 (from the year 2000, age 1–5)

Year	1975	1980	1985	1990	1995	2000	2005	2010	2013
%	10	21	32	40	49	66	77	83	84

Source: National Agency, 2014.

required qualification before they are employed in ECEC institutions. To be employed as a preschool teacher you must have a bachelor's degree. In the first year of employment the preschool teacher must fulfil the requirements to obtain authorisation. This means that there is a mentor for new preschool teachers who will ensure that they have the competencies and skills to fulfil tasks in preschool. For carers (or educator assistants) a high school diploma in a programme for work with children and young people is required. Sometimes other educational experiences and diplomas can be validated for carers.

Critical questions

Sweden has a long history of a commitment to degree-qualified staff working with young children, something that is not present in all countries.

» *Do you think that a degree is necessary to work with young children?*

» *In what ways can a degree develop an individual to become an early childhood pedagogue? Are there any particular aspects of a degree that you feel are important?*

CASE STUDY

Stefan

Stefan left his teacher training five years ago without taking a diploma. After working as a personal assistant he decided to take up his studies to become a preschool teacher. He has always been interested in music – he plays guitar in a band – and the preschool training with a music profile was exactly what he was looking for. The training includes guitar playing, choir singing, music subject theory and music didactic. Stefan wishes to work in an ordinary preschool to develop children's music experiences, their creativity and playful learning. He is convinced that aesthetics should be a core subject for all children in preschool.

From philanthropy to social policy for welfare: the early pioneers

The expansion of preschool has in large measure been affected and obstructed by the fact that, apart from offering a field for a largely female workforce, it was also an equality project which enabled both women and men to work outside the home. This has been relevant both in the history of preschool from a Swedish perspective and in the international discussion in recent decades (Letablier and Jönsson, 2005; Scheiwe and Willekens, 2009). Its first phase can be summed up in the words 'From philanthropy to social politics'.

With the more organised, Fröbel-inspired kindergarten movement, established in Sweden from the 1890s and during the first three decades of the twentieth century, there was greater uniformity in form and content. This was supported by the establishment of the first training colleges around 1900, by a common journal, and by an interest association. Together these networks and associations created a distinct ECEC paradigm with targets, content, working methods and pedagogical outlooks, parental co-operation and a relationship to school which had a powerful impact that is still reflected in the present day.

In the construction of the Swedish preschool system and the professions that were developed in relation to preschool, *education* had a central position. Swedish training colleges for kindergarten leaders and child rearers (known as *barnträdgårdsledarinnor* and *uppfostrarinnor*) were founded, displaying close similarities to comparable colleges in many places in both Europe and the USA. The teaching involved working with children in groups, and theory and practice were linked. In the practical work the professional content, professional culture and values were passed on to the younger generations of women. One aim of the training was precisely to influence the young female pupil. It was not just knowledge that had to be acquired; a distinct new identity was to be shaped, where kindergarten teachers could recognise each other whether they were working in Sweden, another Nordic country, or elsewhere in Europe. This identity was stronger than just being a professional identity, it was something that followed a person through life. The kindergarten teachers controlled for a long time the content, scope and organisation of the education at the training colleges. Women occupied all positions in the field until the time when the state took over in the 1960s, which was remarkably late in the history of education. This was of major strategic significance for the professionalisation process in the field, and above all for the professionalisation of preschool teachers. The colleges included several forms of education, which often built on each other and were geared to upbringing in the home, to working as a children's nurse in homes or institutions, or becoming a kindergarten leader/teacher. Internal solidarity was emphasised and open division was to be avoided. The significance of the training for work with younger children was clearly stressed. It was an early and highly explicit professionalisation strategy.

Women at the end of the nineteenth century were excluded from many fields of education, professions and jobs. For a bourgeois woman the home was, broadly speaking, the only possible sphere of work. Motherhood and the home were greatly idealised, and this was where women had their natural place. The main principle was that the sexes were essentially different, and this applied in particular to the more privileged classes. Women and men were perceived differently and had to be kept separate, with moral and hygienic arguments to support this (Fröbel, 1982). The kindergarten movement did not challenge this, but it broadened the concepts to include a wider social and pedagogical home, and to include a wider social, societal and spiritual form of motherhood (Key, 1914; Allen, 1991). The female teachers were also given a great many different designations clearly related to the concept of the family, such as *skolmoster* (school aunt), *skolmamsell* (school mademoiselle) and *fröken* (miss).

Through their social and educational tasks in care, nursing and education, free zones of a kind were created for women, gradually developing into occupations and semi-professions.

Here the women created areas which were affected by the female group's cultural and class gender, which was regarded as *nature*, and thus established these fields of work. This simultaneously meant an indirect social exclusion of men (Havung, 2002). There was no active barring of men, but the structure of the field was an activity for women built with a number of markers which in many ways kept men out. From the 1940s to the 1960s, the activities and the training were then associated with municipal and state structures, which affected the composition of the workforce and opened the door to men who could occupy the leading positions in the colleges and elsewhere. Before that, women occupied all positions in the field. The gendered occupational structure nevertheless affected the professions of childcarer and preschool teacher, and the proportion of men, since the training was made open for men in the 1960s, has been around 3–5 per cent. A great many measures and projects have been implemented to change this composition, but there has been very little success (SOU, 2006, p 75).

CASE STUDY

Anna

Anna was in the same group in the teacher training programme as Stefan. She was younger than him and had just finished high school. She knew exactly what she wanted – to work with children. In her family both her mother and older sister worked in caring and nursing jobs, it was a kind of tradition in the family. Anna likes her work as a preschool teacher very much. She works at a preschool focused on outdoor education, and they spend many hours of the week outdoors with the children. There are no men working there, but Anna hopes it will change in the future; however, there are very few men working as preschool teachers. Anna wants to take more courses at the university, especially about science for children and about children at risk. There are very few possibilities to have special work profiles or make a career in preschool, and that bothers Anna.

Critical questions

Sweden is not the only country to have a low number of men working in ECEC.

» *What do you think are the potential barriers to men entering ECEC professions?*

» *What ideas can you come up with to increase the number of men working in ECEC?*

» *What do you think would be the benefits of having more men working in ECEC?*

The early emphasis on training for both childcarers and kindergarten leaders/teachers is crucial for the history of the profession and the early ECEC institution. During the training period a collective identity was created, a professional language, a community of language and values. The identity was marked in different ways, as in the nursing professions, with clothing, dress symbols, caps, brooches and the like which identified both the group as a whole and the college where the individuals were trained. These artefacts also distinguished the childcarer and preschool teacher from the ordinary woman and the mother, even though they often performed exactly the same tasks. Boundary markers became especially important in a profession which was so close to the home and to motherhood. Several of the training colleges were boarding schools. The principals of the colleges had a much broader responsi-bility for the pupils than would exist today. The women in charge of the training colleges had a very strong position for the development of ECEC. The colleges were the power centres of the day, and this was where the curriculum was formulated which would set its stamp on the activity (Tallberg Broman, 1993, 1994; Vallberg Roth, 2006).

Social policy and the modern project: the early establishment of a profession

The state takeover of the training colleges for preschool teachers came remarkably late by Swedish standards, in relation to other teacher training institutions. This has to do with their character of colleges initiated by and for women. Women were not a state responsibility. It was not up to the state to organise and finance this; women's education was something the home – and through the patriarchal rationality the father – should have both the responsibil-ity and the right to control. It was not until 1963 that the first training college for preschool teachers was taken over by the state. The trainee childcarers and kindergarten leaders were supposed to be suitable and knowledgeable. They had to have the requisite personality and education. A female pupil had to have a *calling* for the task. At a time when there was notice-able resistance to the establishment of vocational training for women, the emphasis on an educational calling can be interpreted as a successful strategy for this group by which women could find a way from a private to a more public world.

Through the training colleges and in the unions, as well as through periodicals and networks, the early training and the ECEC activities had international connections. The early develop-ment of ECEC in Sweden was influenced to a large extent by the German Fröbel tradition as it was changed and managed to suit the conditions prevailing in the local national context. During the period when the ECEC institutions were being developed, there was a recurrent critical attitude to family and school alike. This criticism can be understood partly as a stage in a professionalisation process and in the complicated establishment of the space for a new institution for younger children, between two such firmly established institutions as home and school. It was between these that ECEC was created, as an institution that simultan-eously threatened the home and parenthood and challenged ideas about the needs and interests of young children.

In the 1930s scientific argumentation became increasingly prominent as a foundation for the professionals, but with an admixture of and interaction with discourses that had been active in earlier periods. A period of expansion and development began, but it came to an end in the years of crisis and war in the 1940s, which were followed by a very home-centred period in the 1950s.

In the 1950s, the conflict between the state's interest in increasing labour market participa-tion among mothers of young children and the needs of the child was considered by a com-mittee on family policy (SOU, 1951, p 15). The conclusion was that children under three were best cared for at home by their parents, while they would gain from more collective forms from age three until school age. At the same time, the committee supported society's need for labour and women's freedom of choice to work, and suggested an expansion of childcare institutions for all preschool-age children, although the implicit idea was limited to kindergartens. (Jönsson et al, 2013).

The state and the profession: dilemmas and legitimisation

The main task for daycare centres before the 1960s was to take care of single mothers' children. They were part of child health and an alternative to foster care placement. It was important for the workforce in the ECEC institution to strive for an extended view of the ECEC institution's function in society. A way to do that was to recognise ECEC as a responsibility for the state. At the time, there was a critical discussion about the quality of the private daycare centres and an emerging interest on the part of the state to support alternatives. The state's interest in young children's education and learning was concentrated in preschool, with educational aims and trained personnel. Numerous government inquiries were conducted, more or less explicitly dealing with preschool issues and the building of new ECEC settings. The institutions that were started, however, were local initiatives (Persson, 1998).

Typically, the pedagogical aspects were emphasised in preschool while social aspects were emphasised in daycare centres. This was a controversial issue, and discussions of how to bridge the settings were lively in the preschool teachers association. The different ways to organise ECEC institutions led to a political struggle for professional legitimacy to get policy support and to position the preschool teachers in the professional landscape. Preschool teachers, as part of their professionalisation process, argued that the different settings should be equivalent in educational purposes. Preschool teachers have historically regarded care and education as inseparable and have argued that an educational activity led by trained preschool teachers was needed 'for the sake of the children' (Tallberg Broman, 1994). The striving for professional legitimisation was in this perspective two-fold: on the one hand constructing a partnership with parents and caregivers in the child's interest and, on the other hand, claiming that professional knowledge and competence were needed to combine education and care.

Critical questions

There is much debate about the interplay between care and education in ECEC.

» *Draw two circles, one to represent care, the other education. You can overlap the circles as much or as little as you like, but consider why you have drawn them as you have.*

» *Have you drawn your circles the same size? Does this reflect how you see care or education as being more important?*

Whether or not childcare should operate in the public sector was a major issue during these decades. The increased demand for a growing labour force was a reason for the state to build new ECEC institutions. Yet the dominant view from the past was strongly influenced by an ideology of the family and women's role and function in society as a whole. This discourse claimed that the education and upbringing of young children is a private affair and not a public responsibility.

The recognition of ECEC as a public matter presupposes the execution of the services by qualified professionals, leaving aside the idea that child education and care are the exclusive prerogative of women, seen as mothers, who therefore do not require professional skills (Haddad, 2001). The state interest in the expansion of ECEC broke with the philanthropic idea; now taxes and fees were to finance preschool. It was the state that took responsibility for the content of early childhood education and its organisation. The political need for female labour and the scientific approach to ECEC served as reconciling factors between the various political parties and created a consensus on the core objectives.

From social pedagogy to school readiness

During the 1970s, the model for modern Swedish ECEC was created. All forms of municipal childcare increased significantly during this period. Preschool content was based on theories of cognitive development, psychodynamic development and socialisation. Traditions from kindergarten were integrated with the perception of the individual child and a dialogic pedagogical approach. The content and scientific approach to ECEC advocated a focus on education and well-trained preschool teachers. Half of the workforce in preschool were carers, but it was supposed that carers would be replaced with exclusively preschool teachers in the long run. The two occupations, with respect to their different training and knowledge, were supposed to work in teams. Care and education were to be integrated with each other and performed by all staff in preschool regardless of occupation and salary.

The university reform of 1977 formalised the requirement that education for welfare state professions such as preschool teachers should belong to the academy in university/college. This was in line with the professional ambitions of the preschool teachers. The ambition to integrate care and education in a professional knowledge base required a professional profile that could fulfil both educational and social functions. Scientific and academic knowledge constitutes a base for professionalisation, and the academic training made it possible for preschool teachers to claim that their professional knowledge was crucial for achieving the goals and objectives in preschool.

Since the 1990s, preschool has been seen as the first stage of lifelong learning, which is emphasised in the recent reforms of preschool along with the importance of the inclusion of all groups of young children, including children of unemployed and of migrant background. The transfer of the responsibility from the Ministry of Health and Welfare to the Ministry of Education (1996) emphasised its role in an educational context. In 2008 the Swedish National Agency for Education asked for a revision of the 1998 curriculum with the aim of increasing the role of language, mathematics, natural science and technology to prepare children for school. The revised curriculum was introduced in 2010 with a multidiscursive approach to learning and value-embedded education.

As shown above, a significant aspect of Swedish and Nordic ECEC policy is the idea of sharing child education and care between families and public institutions (Karila, 2012). The professional and political struggle for legitimisation of early childhood education was based on the acceptance of shared responsibility for young children's socialisation and education. The model of Social Pedagogy is successful in this respect, with the intention to interconnect education and care, encouraging play, relationship, curiosity and the desire for meaning-making based on activities that value both children and educators in a co-constructing environment (Karila, 2012). Scandinavian researchers have described it as the Nordic model for organising ECEC, with emphasis on children's participation, democracy and autonomy. It has been concluded that it is an educational philosophy that stresses psychological and social development rather than formal instruction (Jensen, 2009; Jensen et al, 2010). In an international context, the contemporary Swedish preschool is often held up as a good model of educare, that is a preschool that includes both good-quality care and education (OECD, 2001, 2006; Moss, 2006).

Tensions and politics

The development of ECEC institutions in Sweden has in this chapter been described through the lenses of gender and professionalisation processes. Finally we would like to discuss some tensions between history and politics.

Women's increased participation in the labour market from the 1970s onwards was made possible by a large female collective taking over much of the work of caring for and teaching young children. A national redistribution of these tasks was carried out within the female collective.

There has been much less redistribution of work between the sexes as regards to the responsibility for and care of children. The women in the Swedish example escaped economic dependence on men, to become instead dependent on a new partner, the state, as a guarantor of welfare services, such as childcare. In a time of restructuring and economic decline, the fragility of this equation has become increasingly obvious. In combination with equality in working life according to a model for work which was designed for male employees in a time when other forms of family existed, and with the male model as the norm, this has had negative repercussions for the female collective and for the fields for which women have had special responsibility. This is reflected in the gender distribution of the ECEC workforce, despite several attempts to adjust the ratio of men and women working in ECEC.

Problematic gender assumptions which view masculinity as natural and less changeable, beyond social influence and control, and woman as changeable and adaptable, have been interwoven in the prevailing gender regimes (Hearn, 1998). An increased interest in the equal man has however come into focus in recent years. In Swedish public inquiries concerning equality policy in the 1990s and the 2000s there is a greater interest in including both men and women in gainful employment and in work with the home and children. Interestingly, the Swedish assistant minister of education is responsible for both preschool and equality.

Critical reflections: welfare professions in the new era

In the era of globalisation and dominant economic discourses, the professional's struggle for legitimacy and cultural recognition in society takes place in a new context.

ECEC in Sweden is now highly recognised as an important institution for children's early learning and socialisation but there are growing demands for efficiency, new standards and quality development. The discourse of a lifelong learning paradigm (Biesta, 2006) influences all parts of the educational system and puts new and, in relation to tradition, contradictory demands on the workforce in ECEC. As a consequence, the model of Social Pedagogy has been criticised for being too focused on social aspects of children's learning and not using its full potential to stimulate children's academic learning. This transformation of ECEC may be seen as a process of professionalisation and recognition in the educational system but it is also evident that it is a top-down process that leads to a 'pedagogical and professional uncertainty' in a hierarchical educational system. It is a major challenge for the preschool teachers (and the carers) in Swedish ECEC to develop a professional language and a common base of knowledge in the new era (Persson and Tallberg Broman, 2013).

Further reading

Lohmander, M K (2004) The Fading of a Teaching Profession? Reforms of Early Childhood Teacher Education in Sweden. *Early Years*, 24(1): 23–34.

This journal article supports the chapter here in the overview that it provides on changes in ECEC in Sweden through history. It then considers in more detail the development of integrated teaching degrees.

Campaign: More men in preschool

The National Agency started a new campaign to recruit men to preschool in 2014. It includes national conferences throughout the country, advertising, films and a brochure (www.skolverket.se/om-skolverket/om-oss/kampanj-fler-man-i-forskolan-1.212793, accessed 28 November 2014).

References

Allen, A T (1991) *Feminism and Motherhood in Germany 1800–1914*. New York: Rutgers University Press.

Biesta, G (2006) *Beyond Learning: Democratic Education for a Human Future*. Herndorn: Paradigm Publishers.

Fröbel, F W A (1887) *The Education of Man*. New York: Appleton.

Fröbel, F W A (1982) *Kommt, lasst uns unsern kindern leben*. Band 1–3. Berlin: Volk und Wissen. Volkseigener verlag.

Haddad L (2001) An Integrated Approach to Early Childhood Education and Care: A Preliminary Study. Paper presented at International Conference on Early Childhood Education and Care. Stockholm.

Havung, M (2002) *Anpassning till rådande ordning: en studie av manliga förskollärare i förskoleverksamhet. [Adapting to the Prevailing Order: A Study of Male Preschool Teachers in Early Childhood Education]*. Malmö: Studia psychologica et paedagogica. Series altera, 145.

Hearn, J, Edwards, J, Popay J and Oakley A (1998) Introduction: The Trouble with Men, in Popay, I J, Hern, J and Edwards, J (eds) *Men, Gender Divisions and Welfare*. London: Routledge, ss 1–8.

Hernes, H (1987) *Welfare State and Women Power. Essays in State Feminism*. Oslo: Norwegian University Press.

Jensen, B (2009) A Nordic Approach to Early Childhood Education (ECE) and Socially Endangered Children. *European Early Childhood Education Research Journal*, 17: 7–21.

Jensen, A S, Broström, S and Hansen, O H (2010) Critical Perspectives on Danish Early Childhood Education and Care: Between the Technical and the Political. *Early Years*, 30: 243–54.

Jönsson, I, Sandell, A and Tallberg Broman, I (2013) Change or Paradigm Shift in the Swedish Preschool? *Journal Sociologia, Problemas e Práticas*, 69: 47–62.

Karila, K (2012) A Nordic Perspective of Early Childhood Education and Care Policy. *European Journal of Education*, 47(4): 2012.

Key, E (1914) *Missbrukad kvinnokraft och Kvinnopsykologi*. (4:de upplagan). Stockholm: Bonniers.

Letablier, M-T and Jönsson, I (2005) The Logic of Public Action, in Gerhard, U, Knijn, T and Weckwert, A (eds) *Working Mothers in Europe: A Comparison of Policies and Practices*. Cheltenham: Edward Elgar Publishing Ltd., pp 41–57.

Moss, P (2006) From a Childcare to a Pedagogical Discourse – or Putting Care in Its Place, in Lewis, J (ed), *Children, Changing Families and Welfare States*. Cheltenham: Edward Elgar Publishing Ltd, pp 154–72.

National Agency (2014) *Children and Staff in Preschool*. Stockholm: National Agency.

Nauman, I (2005) Child Care and Feminism in West Germany and Sweden in the 1960s and the 1970s. *Journal of European Social Policy*, 15(1): 47–63.

OECD (1996) *Lifelong Learning for All*. Meeting of the Education Committee at the Ministerial Level, 16–17 January 1996. Paris: OECD.

OECD (2001) *Starting Strong: Early Childhood Education and Care*. Paris: OECD.

OECD (2006) *Starting Strong II: Early Childhood Education and Care*. Paris: OECD.

Ozga, J and Jones, R (2006) Travelling and Embedded Policy: The Case of Knowledge Transfer. *Educational Policy*, 32(1): 1–17.

Persson, S (1998) *Förskolan i ett samhällsperspektiv* [Preschool in a Societal Perspective]. Lund: Studentlitteratur.

Persson, S and Tallberg Broman, I (2013) ECEC in the Scandinavian Countries – In Transformation from National Welfare Policy to Global Economy and Learning? Paper presented at EECERA conference. Talinn.

Randall, V (1995) Feminism and Child Daycare. *Journal of Social Politics*, 25(4): 485–505.

Scheiwe, K and Willekens, H (2009) Introduction, in Scheiwe, K and Willekens, H (eds) *Childcare and Preschool Development in Europe: Institutional Perspectives*. Basingstoke: Palgrave.

SOU (1951: 15) *Daghem Och Skolor. Betänkande om Barnstugor och Barntillsyn. Avgivet av 1946 års Kommitté för den Halvöppna Barnavården*, Stockholm: Socialdepartementet.

SOU (2006:75) *Jämställdhet i förskolan* [Equality in Preschool]. Stockholm: Utbildningsdepartementet.

Statistics Sweden (2013) *Förskola – barn och grupper – riksnivå Preschool – children and groups – national level*. Stockholm: Statistiska centralbyrån.

Tallberg Broman, I (1993) *When Work Was Its Own Reward: A Swedish Study from the Perspective of Women's History of the Kindergarten Teacher as Public Educator*. Malmö: Malmö University.

Tallberg Broman, I (1994) *Gender Perspectives on the Formation of the Professional Field for Caring and Education of Children*. Malmö: Malmö University.

Vallberg Roth, A-C (2006) Early Childhood Curricula in Sweden – from the 1850s to the Present. *International Journal of Early Childhood*, 38(1): 77–98.

6 The Australian ECEC workforce: feminism, feminisation and fragmentation

FRANCES PRESS

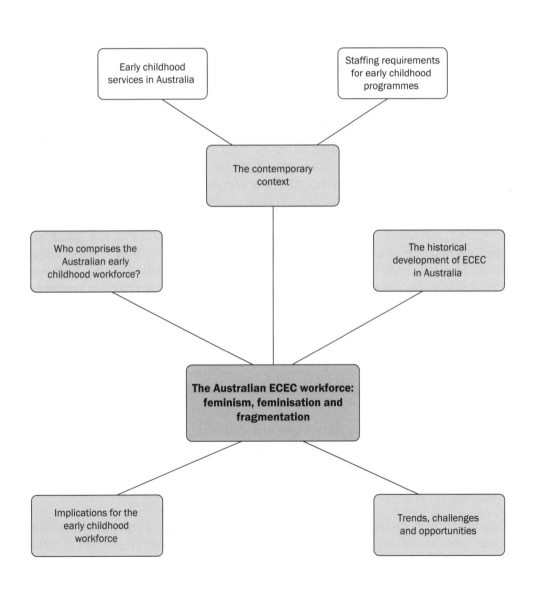

Introduction

This chapter examines the Australian early childhood education and care (ECEC) workforce: its composition, history and challenges. In doing so, it identifies and analyses key influences upon the nature of the workforce including its highly feminised nature as well as the various positionings and discursive shifts that have characterised Australian ECEC policy since the inception of the Australian kindergarten movement in the late 1800s.

The chapter commences with a brief overview of the Australian context: geographically, demographically and politically. This is followed by an examination of the specific policy context for ECEC and a précis of workforce characteristics. The chapter then examines historical and contemporary factors that have served to shape the workforce in particular ways. It concludes by elucidating current debates and challenges.

In reading this chapter, it is important to note that in September 2013, Australia elected a new national government. This government has signalled its intention to slow down the pace of wide-ranging early childhood policy reform introduced by the previous Labor government after its election in 2007. Over time, it is expected this slow down will have an impact on the nature of the early childhood workforce.

The contemporary context

Australia's population is concentrated along its coast lines, especially the east coast, and within its state and territory capital cities. However, there is also a significant inland population with many Australians living in regional, rural and remote parts of the country. Because the country is so large, many people living in rural areas have to travel significant distances to reach townships with services for young children, and distance has given rise to innovation. In 1951, the School of the Air was started to give children in remote areas access to school education over shortwave radio. Still operating today, it uses wireless computer technology to reach children living in remote areas where the population is not large enough to locate a school. For younger children, mobile children's services ('mobiles') deliver early childhood programmes to remote townships and farms. These vans packed with equipment and resources can, in some regions, be on the road for weeks at a time.

Critical questions

» *Considering Australia's geographical expanse, what do you think about the idea of education via the internet?*

» *What do you think are the advantages and disadvantages of this model?*

» *Do you think this model works for all children (think about age and ability)?*

» *How important a feature do you think the 'mobiles' are for supporting online learning?*

Australia is culturally diverse. In 2013, almost 28 per cent (or 6.4 million) of the resident population was estimated to have been born overseas with a further 20 per cent of residents having at least one parent born overseas. Cultural diversity and the need for early childhood services to respond to the needs of migrant families has long been a focus for Australian ECEC. In the early 1950s, in response to high levels of post-war European migration, the Australian Pre-school Association (APA – previously known as the Australian Association for Pre-school Child Development); in the 1980s it became the Australian Early Childhood Association and is now known as Early Childhood Australia) lobbied successfully for the provision of English classes for mothers in migrant hostels while their children were minded by qualified preschool teachers. With the rapid expansion of childcare services in the last three decades of the twentieth century, the necessity of culturally inclusive and responsive early childhood programmes has been foregrounded by advocacy groups and providers of professional support (Press and Wong, 2013). Today respect for cultural diversity is a principle embedded in the national curriculum framework (DEEWR, 2009a).

When Australia became a federation in 1901, legislative powers were divided between the states and the national government (see Wong and Press, 2015 for further details on the history of Australian colonies). In a division of power that has particular relevance to ECEC, the constitution granted the states responsibility for education while the national government had responsibility for welfare. This division of powers served to shape the early childhood sector and its workforce in distinct ways over the ensuing century.

Early childhood services in Australia

ECEC services can be home-based or centre-based and provide either short or long day services. They may be managed by non-profit entities such as community-based associations, local government or government departments (the latter is more common in relation to traditional preschool services), or commercial organisations. To assist in understanding the configuration of services that make up the Australian early childhood sector, *preschool* in Table 6.1 is defined in its traditional sense as a sessional stand-alone service. However, recent reforms have blurred the policy distinction between childcare (long daycare) and preschool, and the provision of preschool is now considered an education and care programme delivered by a qualified early childhood teacher. Under the Early Childhood Reform Agenda (DEEWR, 2009a) introduced by the former federal Labor government (2007–13) both long daycare centres and preschools are required to employ teachers with early childhood qualifications.

Staffing requirements for early childhood programmes

Currently, all formal early childhood services must meet the standards established by the Australian Children's Education and Care Quality Authority (ACECQA). These encompass specific requirements for staff which are outlined in Tables 6.2–6.4. All early childhood qualified staff working directly with children, irrespective of level of qualification or whether they are working in a centre-based setting or family daycare, are referred to as *educators*. To gain employment in ECEC educators must hold, or be working toward, a qualification, although this is a relatively recent requirement. Three types of qualification are mandated, each associated with different roles and responsibilities, conditions and rates of pay.

Table 6.1 Service types

Family daycare (FDC)	Care and education provided in the educator's home. Educators must be registered with a family daycare co-ordination unit which is responsible for approving people to operate as family daycare educators, as well as providing ongoing support, training and advice to educators. There are approximately 450 FDC co-ordination units (National Family Daycare Association, nd).
Long daycare (LDC) (Also childcare)	Centre-based programmes operating for a minimum of 8 hours a day for 48 weeks of the year. Children can attend for up to 50 hours a week, but the average usage is 27.5 hours (DEEWR, 2013).
Preschool (PS)	Preschools offer sessional programmes (ie, a morning or afternoon session, or a short day eg, 6 hours) for children in the year or two before they commence school. In some jurisdictions preschools are part of the state/territory education system and often co-located with schools. However, there are considerable variations to this pattern. The Early Childhood Reform Agenda (2009) aimed to make 15 hours per week of preschool education available to every child in the year before school. This preschool programme may be delivered in a traditional stand-alone preschool, or within a long daycare centre.
Integrated child and family programmes (integrated services)	These include early childhood education and care programmes and other supports to families such as maternal child health and family support. The suite of services offered is highly dependent on context.
Mobile children's services	Mobile services are travelling children's services, operating out of a bus or van that serve rural, isolated or disadvantaged communities. The services offered vary according to location, but may include play sessions, preschool programmes, long daycare programmes, or childminding while parents attend another activity.

Table 6.2 Mandated minimum staff to child ratios

Staff to child ratios	
Centre-based education and care (eg, long daycare and preschool)	
Birth to 24 months	1 educator to 4 children
Over 24 months and less than 36 months	1 educator to 5 children
36 months of age and less than school age (generally age 5)	1 educator to 11 children
Family daycare (one educator)	
No more than 7 children in total	
No more than 4 children preschool age or under	

Table 6.3 Mandated minimum requirements for qualified staff

Qualified staff	
Centre-based education and care (eg, long daycare and preschool)	
Fewer than 25 children	Access to an early childhood teacher (ECT) for at least 20% of the time that the service operates.
25 or more but less than 60 children	1 ECT
60 or more but less than 80 children	2 ECTs. The 2nd teacher must be in attendance: • at least 3 hours a day, if the service operates for 50 or more hours a week; or • 30% of the operating hours of the service on that day, if the service operates for less than 50 hours a week.
More than 80 children	2 ECTs. The 2nd teacher must be in attendance: • at least 6 hours a day, if the service operates for 50 or more hours a week; or • 60% of the operating hours of the service on that day, if the service operates for less than 50 hours a week.
• At least 50% of educators must have, or be actively working towards, an approved diploma. • All other educators must have, or be actively working towards, a certificate III.	
Family daycare	
• Family daycare educators must have a certificate III. • Family daycare co-ordinators must have a diploma.	

Table 6.4 Types of qualification

Early Childhood Teaching Qualification	A three or four year university degree with an early childhood teaching specialisation. Degrees often cover the age ranges from birth to five years; birth to eight years; or birth to twelve years.
Diploma in Early Childhood Education and Care	A two-year vocational qualification undertaken at a Recognised Training Organisation. Requires the completion of High School (to Year 12) or mature age entry.
Certificate III in Early Childhood Education and Care	A one-year certificate from a Recognised Training Organisation. Requires completion of High School to an intermediate level (Year 10).

Who comprises the Australian early childhood workforce?

Ninety-seven per cent of the early childhood workforce are women. The workforce is increasing, with both long daycare and preschool growing from 52,105 and 10,321 respectively in 2004 to 67,975 and 25,475 in 2010. When figures include those employed in outside school hours care, the workforce almost doubled between 1997 and 2010. The area experiencing decline is family daycare with the number of family daycare educators slowly reducing over time from 15,700 educators in 1997 to 13, 575 in 2010 (Productivity Commission, 2011). Almost half the workforce are employed in long daycare, with a much smaller percentage (17.6 per cent) working in preschool and just under 10 per cent in family daycare. Most of those employed in preschools and FDC (almost two-thirds) are over 40 years of age (Social Research Centre, 2014).

Since the introduction of the Early Childhood Reform Agenda, all educators working in early childhood programmes must hold a qualification (Table 6.4). This has not always been the case and in 2001 less than half of staff in children's services (including outside-school-hours care services) were qualified (Tasman Economics, 2001). The majority of educators hold a certificate III or a certificate IV (44.4 per cent in 2013), or a diploma or advanced diploma (40.1 per cent in 2013). A much smaller percentage hold a bachelor's degree (15.5 per cent), mainly in early childhood education (Productivity Commission, 2014).

Critical questions

»   *Australia is not the only country to have variation in the qualification levels of those working in ECEC. What do you think of this variation in qualification levels?*

»   *Do you think everyone should have the same qualification level? Why?*

»   *What level of qualification do you think should be the minimum requirement to work with children? Would you vary this by the age of the child?*

The historical development of ECEC in Australia

> *By late in the century a formidable network of women was working in support of feminist causes – divorce law reform, votes for women, equal pay for equal work – and for education of the poor, setting up 'Ragged Schools' in the 1860s and the Free Kindergartens and the Kindergarten Union in the 1890s.*
>
> (Huntsman, 2005, p 9)

The historical foundation of Australian ECEC in philanthropy and educational reform resulted in workforce preparation for the early childhood sector being distinct from, and for much of its history independent of, teacher training for the school sector. The earliest advocates of early childhood education (kindergarten) in Australia were often feminists concerned with social reform, including educational reform. Although many early advocates regarded the establishment of kindergartens as a philanthropic endeavour, a means by which to keep working class children off the street and to curb the threat of *larrikinism* (quoted as: '*Cowards they are to the marrow of their bones. Lazy they are in bone and marrow, drunken, dissolute and thievish.*'

In the *Advertiser* 17 August 1901: 6) they were also keen to reform and improve teaching in school education. In 1893, Sir George Houston Reid (MP), declared that kindergarten

> *converted what used to be a barbarous system of learning into a system of education which makes education a positive delight and a source of strength to those children who are taught by it.*

(1893, p 6740)

Margaret Windeyer, a feminist, travelled to the United States in the 1890s where she befriended the prominent American philosopher and educational reformer, John Dewey, who himself was interested in, and influenced by, the educational ideas of Frederich Froebel. Following a visit to the Golden Gate Kindergarten Association, she brought back to Australia its annual report. This report inspired her friend, fellow suffragette and educational reformer, Maybanke Wolstenholme (later Anderson) who found the Kindergarten Union of New South Wales, the first kindergarten association in Australia (Brennan, 1998). The objectives of this Kindergarten Union included the establishment of free kindergartens in poor neighbour-hoods and the introduction of the principles of kindergarten education in every school in New South Wales (Roberts, 1997, p 110).

Kindergarten Unions (or their equivalent) were soon formed in other Australian colonies (then states). Their formation was closely followed by the establishment of kindergarten teacher training institutions, the Kindergarten Teachers Colleges (KTCs). These were independent from the State Teachers Colleges and their courses were usually of longer duration (three years) (Press and Wong, 2013). Kindergarten advocates considered it imperative to have staff trained in kindergarten methods and until such time as Australia produced its own graduates, the newly formed kindergartens were headed by teachers from Britain and the United States (Brennan, 1998).

Although many free kindergartens were set up in poor neighbourhoods, Kindergarten Unions were opposed to mothers being in paid employment and refused to provide care to children under three or extended hours of care. In the early 1900s, concern for the welfare of chil-dren whose mothers had to work, triggered the emergence of the day nursery movement. Eventually, day nursery associations started their own training institutions, as kindergarten training colleges eschewed the need to provide training for infants and very young children on the grounds that their students were *to be 'trained as teachers not nurses'* (Brennan, 1998, p 26). Training for day nursery staff was initially modelled on nursing and had a strong focus on health and hygiene. Over time, day nurseries began to include larger numbers of older children (age two to five) and so the Sydney Day Nursery Association, inspired by the spe-cialist nursery school training in the United Kingdom, established a Nursery School Teachers College in 1932 (Huntsman, 2013).

These foundational years instituted strong philosophical splits that were to characterise the preparation of the early childhood workforce for years to come:

- an early childhood teaching identity distinct from that of teacher preparation for schools, with a strong emphasis on child development, child study and kindergarten methods; and

- an ideological split between the kindergarten movement and the day nursery movement.

For the first half of the twentieth century such ECEC services primarily remained as philanthropic concerns. In the latter half of the century, 'preschool' (kindergarten) began to appeal to middle-class families, who agitated for the provision of parent run preschools in their communities. However, it was not until the 1960s that preschools attracted significant attention from a number of state and territory departments of education. The Victorian government already funded preschools (kindergartens) through its Department of Health, largely through the efforts of the Director of Maternal, Infant and Preschool Welfare, Dr Vera Scantlebury Brown, in the 1940s, but this trend was not evident in other jurisdictions. Once more, developments in Australia were sparked by trends in the United Kingdom and the United States. Both the Plowden Report (United Kingdom) and Project Headstart (United States) had pointed to the role of preschool in improving children's outcomes in school. Such findings stimulated a number of Australian education departments to become more actively involved in preschool provision (Press and Wong, 2013). Notwithstanding this early interest, there is still considerable variation today in the extent to which preschools are directly provided by state education departments. It is only relatively recently that early childhood policy has aimed for a national entitlement to preschool of 15 hours a week the year before school (DEEWR, 2009a).

However, the most significant growth in the provision of ECEC in Australia resulted from the introduction of the Commonwealth *Child Care Act 1972*, a highly significant reform that enabled the national government to invest in childcare on a large scale. The Child Care Act was triggered by the confluence of three trends: increasing concern for young children who were left at home alone because their mothers needed to work; the women's liberation movement and its accompanying demand for childcare so that mothers could work outside the home; and the need of the manufacturing industry for access to cheap (read women's) labour (Wong and Press, 2015). In the ensuing two decades, childcare expanded as a result of government subsidies enabling the provision of community-based non-profit services. Under neo-liberal economic reforms of the 1990s, fee subsidies were made available to commercial providers and since that time, private, for-profit childcare has dominated Australian centre-based childcare provision. Preschools remain largely a non-profit venture, run by departments of education or parent committees.

Implications for the early childhood workforce

During the early years of childcare expansion, the dichotomy between care and education that had been established in the first half of the twentieth century remained. This dichotomy was further entrenched by the fact that funding for childcare came from the national government and was closely linked to policy objectives related to women's employment and welfare, while funding for preschools (regarded as educational and developmental) rested with the state and territory governments. It took some years for the peak early childhood association to embrace the childcare movement, finally changing its name from the Australian Preschool Association to the Australian Early Childhood Association in the early 1980s.

In the initial years of funding from the national government, subsidies to childcare services were tied to the employment of early childhood teachers. However, many teachers were reluctant to work in childcare – the hours were longer, they received fewer holidays and no time to prepare for teaching. In addition, many early childhood teachers believed that childcare was not good for children. Thus a new type of qualification emerged: the childcare certificate. This was undertaken at a vocational training institution, rather than teachers college, and was the precursor to today's certificates and diploma. As the pull on government expenditure expanded with the growth of childcare places, the government broke the nexus between funding and teacher qualifications (teachers were paid more than childcare workers), converting its subsidy to operational funding. Thus most qualified staff working in childcare centres were not university-qualified teachers.

The fragmentation of the workforce was further embedded through differing union coverage for the early childhood staff. Teachers employed in preschools and childcare centres are mostly covered by education unions, while other early childhood educators are covered by the union now known as United Voice, a union which covers a range of workers in service industries. In a further complication, early childhood staff employed by local government have come under the Municipal Employees Union. This has meant that industrially, early childhood staff have not been united by a single representative body.

In response to, at times, palpable divides, there have been initiatives both by the early childhood field itself and, more recently, through government policy to create a more unified early childhood sector. During the 1980s, the Australian Early Childhood Association made a deliberate effort to provide resources and support to all early childhood programmes and their staff, regardless of type of setting. In 1988, it developed a Code of Ethics for Early Childhood Professionals. The Code was designed to address, at least in part, one of the formal attributes of professional status, that is, adherence to ethical standards (Lyons, 2012) and was a public statement of the professionalism of all those who worked in the early childhood field. Developed through a highly consultative process, it was warmly welcomed by the field (it was revised in 2006). However, no professional body oversees the implementation of the Code and there are no sanctions for breaches. Its coverage of all staff regardless of level of qualification and its lack of enforceability have attracted criticism that it is not a true marker of professional status (Lyons, 2012) but there is little evidence that this critique has gained much traction in the early childhood field itself.

Under the Early Childhood Reform Agenda, instigated by the former national Labor government (2007–13), policy for ECEC shifted out of the welfare/community services portfolio into education, and this trend was followed in many state and territory jurisdictions that sought cohesion between childcare and preschool policy. Such policy shifts symbolised the Reform Agenda's intent to create a more unified system, although ironically early childhood education and childcare ended up divided between two ministers. Additionally, it sought to raise the quality of early childhood programmes across the country through whole government agreements involving state/territory and national governments. As part of these reforms, the Australian Children's Education and Care Quality Authority (ACECQA) was established. ACECQA administers the National Quality Framework (NQF) that monitors standards (the National Quality Standard) for all early childhood programmes regardless of type. A significant initiative under the NQF has been the development and introduction of a national curriculum framework for early childhood, the Early Years Learning Framework (EYLF). This framework covers all early years services. A key plank of the policy that underpins improving the quality of care and education standards has been to raise the requirements for qualified staff.

Trends, challenges and opportunities

Ailwood (2007) reminds us that early childhood education is deeply imbued by the discourse of maternalism and there is no doubt that many of the challenges facing the early childhood workforce are linked to the fact that it is a predominantly female workforce. Early childhood advocates have long had to counteract the perception that caring for young children is an easy job and an extension of women's natural mothering instincts. This perception has led to inequalities in status that are reflected in the pay and conditions of the Australian early childhood workforce, regardless of type of qualification or the positions in which early childhood staff are employed, a point made repeatedly in government reports and pay equity cases (for example the Industrial Relations Commission, NSW, 1998).

Critical questions

» *Can you relate to the view that working with children is seen as an extension of mothering? Is this something that you see within your working environment? Who is it that views working with children this way – you, your colleagues, parents, policymakers, children?*

» *What steps do you think are needed to alter this view (if any)?*

To combat the false belief that working in early childhood is a low-skilled occupation advocates have always emphasised the need for staff to be appropriately qualified and have promoted their professional status. This has occurred since the inception of the first kindergarten union in Australia in 1895 and the subsequent establishment of independent teachers colleges. At the first national conference of the newly formed Australian Association for Pre-School Child Development (AAPSCD) in 1939, speakers reinforced the need for trained early childhood teachers and linked this need to appropriately preparing children for a post-war world. During World War II (1939–45), kindergarten teaching was declared a national service and in the plethora of reviews of early childhood policy since that time, advocates have fought hard to retain and extend requirements for staff with relevant specialist qualifications (Press and Wong, 2013). Ironically such advocacy for professionally prepared staff has not always been accompanied by advocacy for appropriate remuneration. In a 1969 NSW industrial hearing, the Commissioner observed that early childhood staff were 'motivated by a desire to make some contribution to community service' and thus not reliant on wages, a position echoing that of the philanthropic organisations that ran kindergartens (cited in Smith and Lyons, 2006). Further, the need for a specialised body of knowledge and skills for ECEC has often come under attack. Take, for example, the assertion of a former federal government finance minister Peter Walsh (finance minister from 1984 to 1990) in the 1990s that the advocacy for teachers in early childhood programmes was intended '*to make even softer the nests of bachelors of early childhood education and their middle-class well-feathered friends*' and that childcare workers were crippling the system with 'creeping credentialism' (cited in Brennan, 2008, np).

Funding arrangements have compounded poor pay and conditions. The majority of ECEC services rely on parents' fees as their main source of funding. Although fees attract a government subsidy adjusted according to family income, there is no direct subsidy for most services for operational costs. Hence, there are pressures to contain fee levels by keeping staffing costs low. Such conditions have contributed to seemingly entrenched shortages of appro-priately qualified staff (see, for example, Tasman Economics, 2001; Warrilow et al, 2002; Department of Family and Community Services (FACS), 2003; Community Services Ministers Advisory Council, 2006; Productivity Commission, 2011). The reports cited attribute staff shortages to low rates of pay relative to equivalent occupations; inadequate or poor working conditions; a lack of public recognition for the complexity of the work; and pressure arising from multiple workplace demands, including administrative burdens.

Most early childhood staff work in long daycare centres and attendance patterns in these services tend to be highly variable and predominantly part-time. The result is that educators must develop relationships with large numbers of children and their families. For instance a small centre providing 30 full-time places may in fact have 90 children attending (Tasman Economics, 2001). High staff turnover is often cited as a problem. Yet accounts of staff turnover in the Australian ECEC workforce are conflicted. Despite the fact that numerous reports in the past have uncovered quite high rates of turnover (for example, FACS, 2003; Community Services Ministers Advisory Council, 2006), the Productivity Commission (2011) *Report on the Early Childhood Development Workforce* concluded that many staff left to take up positions in other early childhood services, rather than leave the profession altogether. Further, it claimed that the average turnover of the ECEC workforce was only slightly higher (15.7 per cent) than that of all occupations (13.1 per cent). The most recent national staff survey (Social Research Centre, 2014) reports that 87 per cent of respondents were satis-fied with their current job. But fewer than half of respondents (48.9 per cent) were satisfied with their pay and conditions.

In its 2011 report, the Productivity Commission wrote that the Early Childhood Reform Agenda

> is likely to be expensive for both governments and parents, as increased staff numbers, and the higher wages anticipated in response to the increase in demand, drive up ECEC service costs.
>
> (p xxiii)

It is perhaps not surprising then that the terms of reference for the more recently commis-sioned *Productivity Commission Inquiry into Childcare and Early Learning* (2013), instigated by the conservative Coalition government (elected 2013) foregrounds childcare's role in support-ing women's workforce participation, making children's outcomes a secondary consideration. This is a very different framing to that put forward by the preceding Reform Agenda. Indeed, the recommendations from the inquiry (Productivity Commission, 2014) split care from the educa-tion of young children; removed the need for staff to have qualifications greater than entry level (Certificare III) to work with children less than two years of age; and increased financial support for families who use nannies at the expense of increased support for a childcare system.

Critical reflections

The history of the early childhood workforce in Australia is one of feminism, feminisation and fragmentation.

Many of the earliest proponents and deliverers of early childhood education were suffragettes, and educational reformers, a 'formidable network of women ... working in support of feminist causes' (Huntsman, 2005). In these earliest years, kindergarten teaching also opened up opportunities for young women's further education and employment. Nevertheless, this was a poorly paid profession, and one deeply imbued with philanthropy. Thus while kindergarten teachers were extolled to obtain, utilise and demonstrate a specialist body of knowledge and skills, they were not encouraged to seek the pay and conditions commensurate with professional work.

In the second half of the twentieth century, feminism again emerged as a driving force for the expansion of early childhood education, as the women's liberation movement sought government support for childcare to enable women's workforce participation. However, this new wave of feminists often found themselves pitted against the descendants of the feminist philanthropists of the original early childhood movement. Deep division emerged between preschool and childcare and this was reflected in the education and preparation of the early childhood workforce.

Set against such fragmentation have been moves to foster a more unified workforce, one that seeks to acknowledge complementarity in difference. Over time, the philanthropic bodies that once sought to keep wages low have instead argued for improved wages and conditions in an effort to sustain a knowledgeable and stable early childhood profession. Initiatives to improve the professional status of all staff, or to provide public recognition of early childhood professionalism, such as the Code of Ethics and the Early Years Learning Framework, have garnered widespread support in the early childhood field. Additionally, the workforce has largely supported reforms aimed at improving the quality of service provision across the board.

However, the early childhood sector in Australia lives in uncertain times. Following the much lauded gains achieved under the Early Childhood Reform Agenda, are two significant reviews: the Productivity Commission Inquiry into Childcare and Early Learning *and the* Review of the National Partnership Agreement on the National Quality Agenda for Early Childhood Education and Care. *The impact of these reviews on the future composition and status of the early childhood workforce are, as yet, unknown.*

Further reading

Brennan, D (1998) *The Politics of Australian Child Care: Philanthropy to Feminism and Beyond* (revised edn). Cambridge University Press: Cambridge.

Brennan's work provides a comprehensive account of the history of Australian early childhood education.

Press, F and Wong, S (2013) *Early Childhood Australia: A voice for children for 75 years*. Canberra: Early Childhood Australia.

Early Childhood Australia is the peak national early childhood body. In its various guises, it has played a key role in shaping and supporting the early childhood sector and workforce. Through its history, the reader can get a sense of the developments and schisms that have helped shape Australian early childhood policy.

References

2014 Review of the National Partnership Agreement on the National Quality Agenda for Early Childhood Education and Care. [online] Available at: www.woolcott.com.au/NQFreview/support-files/2014-Review-Consultation-paper-21-May.pdf (accessed 1 June 2014).

Ailwood (2007) Mothers, Teachers, Maternalism and Early Childhood Education and Care: some historical connections. *Contemporary Issues in Early Childhood*, 8(2): 157–65.

Australian Bureau of Statistics (2013) Migrant Families in Australia. [online] Available at: www.abs.gov.au/ausstats/abs@.nsf/Latestproducts/3416.0Main+Features2Mar+2013 (accessed 1 June 2014).

Brennan, D (1998) *The Politics of Australian Child Care: Philanthropy to Feminism and Beyond* (rev edn). Cambridge: Cambridge University Press.

Brennan, D (November 2008) Reassembling the Child Care Business. *Inside Story*. [online] Available at: http://inside.org.au/reassembling-the-child-care-business/ (accessed 8 December 2014).

Community Services Ministers' Advisory Council (2006) *National Children's Services Workforce Study*. Melbourne: Community Services Ministers' Advisory Council.

Department of Education, Employment and Workplace Relations (DEEWR) (2009a) Being, Belonging & Becoming: The Early Years Learning Framework for Australia. [online] Available at: http://files.acecqa.gov.au/files/National-Quality-Framework-Resources-Kit/belonging_being_and_becoming_the_early_years_learning_framework_for_australia.pdf (accessed 1 June 2014).

Department of Education, Employment and Workplace Relations (DEEWR) (2009b) National Early Childhood Reform Agenda (2009). [online] Available at: www.workforce.org.au/media/38987/deewr%20big%20picture%20presentation%2015%20september%202009.pdf (accessed 1 June 2014).

Department of Education, Employment and Workplace Relations (DEEWR) (August, 2013) Child Care in Australia. [online] Available at: www.mychild.gov.au/documents/docs/Child_Care_In_Australia.pdf (accessed 1 June 2014).

Department of Family and Community Services (2003) *Australian Government Report on the April 2003 Child Care Workforce Think Tank*. Canberra: Department of Family and Community Services.

Huntsman, L (2005) *For the Little Ones, the Best' SDN Children's Services 1905–2005*. Sydney: Hippo Books.

Huntsman, L (2013) The Nursery School Teachers' College. SDN Children's Services. [online] Available at: www.sdn.org.au/downloads/nursery/files/inc/e68154ab68.pdf (accessed 1 June 2014).

The Larrikin as a Type. *Advertiser,* 17 August 1901, p 6. [online] Available at: http://www.slsa.sa.gov.au/manning/adelaide/larrikin/larrikin.htm (accessed 27 November 2014).

Lyons, M (2012) The Professionalization of Children's Services in Australia. *Journal of Sociology*, 48(2): 115–31.

National Family Day Care Association (nd) About Family Day Care. [online] Available at: www.familydaycare.com.au (accessed 1 June 2014).

Press, F and Wong, S (2013) *Early Childhood Australia: A Voice for Children for 75 years*. Canberra: Early Childhood Australia.

Productivity Commission (2011) Early Childhood Development Workforce. Australian Government Productivity Commission Research Report, Melbourne. [online] Available at: www.pc.gov.au/projects/study/education-workforce/early-childhood/report (accessed 1 June 2014).

Productivity Commission (December 2013) Childcare and Early Learning: Productivity Commission Issue Paper. [online] Available at: http://pc.gov.au/__data/assets/pdf_file/0016/130462/childcare-issues.pdf (accessed 1 June 2014).

Productivity Commission (2014) Report on Government Services. Volume B: Child Care, Education and Training. [online] Available at: www.pc.gov.au/gsp/rogs/childcare-education-training (accessed 1 June 2014).

Productivity Commission (2014). *Childcare and Early Learning: Productivity Commission Draft Report*, Canberra: Productivity Commission

Roberts, J (1997) *Maybanke Anderson: Sex, suffrage and social reform*. Sydney: Hale & Iremonger.

Smith, M and Lyons, M (2006) 'Crying wolf? Employers, awards, and pay equity in the New South Wales children's services industry', *Employment Relations Record*. 6 (1): 49–63.

Social Research Centre (2014) 2013 National Early Childhood Education and Care Workforce Census. [online] Available at: docs.education.gov.au/system/files/doc/other/nwc_national_report_final.pdf (accessed 1 June 2014).

Spearitt, P (1979) Child Care and Kindergartens in Australia 1890–1975, in Langford, P and Sebastian P (eds) *Early Education and Care in Australia*. Sydney: Harcourt Brace Jovanovich.

Tasman Economics (2001). *Caring for Australia's Kids in the 21st Century: Enhancing Capacity to Deliver Quality Children's Services*. HESTA Super Fund.

Warrilow, P, Fisher, K, Cummings, K, Sumsion, J and Beckett, C (2002) *Early Childhood Teachers and Qualified Staff*. Sydney: Social Policy Research Centre, University of New South Wales.

Wong, S and Press, F (2015) The Development of Early Childhood Education and Care in Australia, in Ailwood, J, Boyd, W and Theobald, M (eds) *Early Childhood Education and Care in Australia*. Crows Nest: Allen & Unwin.

7 Japan: young female teachers in kindergartens and nursery schools

MANABU SUMIDA

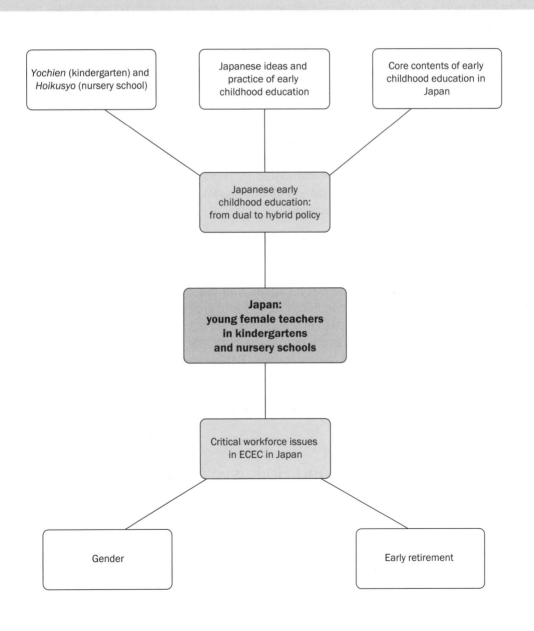

Introduction

In a recent survey of what Japanese children in grade 1 (first year of elementary school; age 6–7 years) want to be in the future, 'nursery teacher' has been a very popular answer as a future job. It was ranked as fifth in 1995, sixth in both 2004 and 2009, and third in 2014 (Kuraray, 2014). In the survey, parents also wanted their children to be a nursery teacher (ranked third in 2014). However, it is the popular choice among grade 1 girls; the results of the survey show that grade 1 boys have never ranked 'nursery teacher' in the top 20 (Kuraray, 2014). The survey asked about preferred job of marriage partner and 'nursery teacher' was very favoured by men but not by women (My navi news, 2013). Thus, the Japanese image of early childhood education and care is stereotypically associated with young females. In this chapter, gender role and early turnover in the context of Japanese kindergartens and nursery schools are discussed with reference to policy and survey results.

In Japan, *Yochien* (kindergartens) were included in a system of national school education under the School Education Act in 1947 and *Hoikusyo* (nursery schools) were identified as a child welfare institution under the Child Welfare Act in the same year. *Yochien* are governed by the Ministry of Education, Culture, Sports, Science and Technology (MEXT) and *Hoikusyo* by the Ministry of Health, Labour and Welfare. The first course of study for kindergarten was mandated in 1956 and has been revised four times up to the present. The first guidelines for childcare at nursery school were mandated in 1965 and revised three times up to the present. In this chapter, the double standards and associated tensions in the Japanese early childhood education will be briefly outlined.

The Japanese language mode of education has a unique tradition, aesthetics and philosophy (Sumida, 2013a). The educational philosophy of Sozo Kurahashi (1882–1955) has long influenced teacher training and educational practice in kindergartens and nursery schools in Japan and this chapter will set out his ideas and practices. In the twenty-first century, Japanese early childhood education is confronted with growing numbers of children on waiting lists for admission to kindergartens and nursery schools, along with issues of urbanisation, nuclearisation of the family, and a drop in the birth rate that emerged in the second half of the twentieth century. In 2014, a new course of study was introduced for a hybrid type of childcare school between kindergarten and nursery school, which is called *Kodomoen*.

Japanese early childhood education: from dual to hybrid policy

Yochien (kindergarten) and *Hoikusyo* (nursery school)

In 1876, the first kindergarten was established by the Ministry of Education in Japan as an institution attached to Tokyo Women's Normal School (now named Ochanomizu Women's University). The childcare provision was strongly influenced by the Fröbel school; Fröbel's *gabe*/gifts were translated into Japanese and incorporated into practice. The establishment of kindergarten was separate from traditional childcare and life conditions in Japan and was the beginning of group learning for the early years. The books *The Kindergarten* written by

Adolf Douai and *A Practical Guide to the English Kindergarten* written by Johannes Ronge were translated into Japanese and strongly influenced Japanese early childhood education.

However, it was not until after World War II that kindergartens were formally recognised as schools. In March 1947, the Education Act and School Education Act came into force and the kindergarten was systemised as part of Japanese school education. Through the Fundamental Law of Education, the School Education Law was promulgated, and the position of kindergarten was established. In December 1947, the Child Welfare Act was enacted, and nursery schools were institutionalised as part of child welfare facilities. This was the starting point for double standards in early childhood education in Japan.

Whereas teachers in kindergarten are identified as a teacher under the School Education Act, teachers in nursery schools are identified as (nationally qualified) workers in childcare, who nurture children in place of their guardians, under the Child Welfare Act. Nursery workers are described in the Child Welfare Act, Article 18, Paragraph 4 as a person who engages in childcare and guides guardians about childcare on the basis of their professional knowledge and skills. The age range of children in kindergartens is from three years to preschool age, and for nursery schools from birth to preschool age.

The nursery was popularly named *Hoikusyo* for a long time, but it was changed to 'nursery' after revision of the Child Welfare Law Enforcement Ordinance of April 1999. In addition, being a nursery worker requires national certification according to the Child Welfare Act amendments of November 2003. Nursery workers had been called *Hobo* (保母) or *Hofu* (保父) but changed to *Hoikushi* (保育士) during the revision of Child Welfare in 1999, and it was in 2003 that *Hoikushi* was identified as a nationally qualified professional.

Every kindergarten must be authorised by the Ministry of Education, Culture, Sports, Science and Technology, and every nursery school must be authorised by the Ministry of Health, Labour and Welfare. These two different institutions are supervised by different legal and fiscal systems. In 2012, three new laws about children and childcare were enacted and a new hybrid educational institution for early years, which is called *comprehensive facilities for early child care and education (幼保連携型認定こども園)*, was established.

The comprehensive facilities for early child care and education was a hybrid between kindergarten as school education and nursery school as childcare. This simplified the supervision and fiscal systems. Behind the new framework lay a number of important issues:

- improvement in the quality of early childhood education;

- enrichment of childcare in all localities;

- elimination of the growing number of children on the waiting list for admission to a kindergarten or nursery school;

- support for local childcare when the number of children decreased;

- consistency between the course of study for kindergartens and the educational guidelines for nursery schools; and

- improvement in the connections between preschool education and primary school education.

For the new hybrid educational institution, there is a new category of teacher *nursery teacher*. The nursery teacher needs to have licences both as a kindergarten teacher and as a child-care professional, and has an important role in promoting the new educational institution.

Critical questions

» *Can you think of any institutions in your own experience that offer comprehensive facilities for early child care and education?*

» *What issues lie behind the establishment of such institutions?*

Japanese ideas and practice of early childhood education
CASE STUDY

Sozo Kurahashi

Sozo Kurahashi has had a significant impact on the ideas and practices of early childhood education in Japan. He was the founder and first president of the Japan Society of Research on Early Childhood Care and Education. After becoming Principal of Tokyo Women's Normal School Kindergarten, he emphasised the importance of natural life and cherished the every-day life of the child. He prepared toys that young children could play with freely, rejecting the formality of Fröbel's principles. He advocated that early childhood education should educate 'from life to life', or 'learning from life', also known as 'guided nursery' (誘導保育論). The principle has been adopted and remains fundamental to Japan thinking up to the present day (The Editorial Committee of Child Care Workers Training, 2007).

Kurahashi identified four characteristics of early childhood education (Sakamoto, 2008). These are:

*   to respect young children's spontaneous life;

*   to be appropriate for collaborative living;

*   to ensure cohesion between aspects of children's lives; and

*   to be emotional rather than conceptual or ideological.

Early childhood education in Japan has the characteristics of spontaneous, interactive, concrete and emotional aspects which all overlap. While Kurahashi was introduced to the work of the Macmillan sisters and Montessori, he had a strong interest in the progressive kindergarten of P S Hill in the USA. He was seeking a new form of childcare rooted in the life and culture of Japanese children (The New Editorial Committee of Child Care Workers Training, 2014).

Kurahashi developed the first systematic curriculum for young children in Japan, known as *Practices of Systematic Child Care Plan* in 1935. This curriculum includes teaching strategies for self-enhancement, enriching teaching, guidance and instruction. The guided nursery plan in the systematic curriculum was an integrated activity plan based on educationally valued themes to establish a bridge between children's free play and culture, to help children make this transition smoothly. The guided nursery sets a theme to encourage children's interest in life through integrated and holistic activities. Large projects were sometimes used with a long timeframe, and themes prepared to make continuous connections with children's lives (Sakamoto, 2008). The guided nursery plan had an introduction (motivation), construction/process, completion and application. The nursery in Tokyo Women's Normal School Kindergarten proposed interesting examples of themes such as, making toys, creating a town, train, doll house, and zoo and these spread all over Japan (The New Editorial Committee of Childcare Workers Training, 2014).

Kurahashi considered that the nursery curriculum was neither objective cultural heritage, nor knowledge and technology, but something to be created through the interaction between a children's life and the nursery worker's life (Suwa, 2007). The philosophy of Kurahashi was founded in the tradition of early childhood education and care as home education, which was expanded to public education. Kurahashi's legacy of early childhood education as a support for home education is deeply rooted in early childhood education of modern Japan.

Critical questions

» *Can you see any parallels between Kurahashi's curriculum created through the interaction between nursery worker and child, and the Vygoskian notion of zone of proximal development (see Chapter 3 for a reminder of what this is)?*

» *What implications does Kurahashi's concept of the co-created curriculum have for training nursery workers?*

Core contents of early childhood education in Japan

The Ministry of Education enacted the course of study for kindergarten in 1956, and prescribed six educational contents fields as health, society, nature, language, music rhythm and arts. After seven years, in 1965, the Ministry of Welfare brought in educational guidelines for childcare and prepared the same six educational contents for up to three-year-old children based on the course of study for kindergarten. The course of study for kindergarten has been revised four times in 1964, 1989, 1989 and 2008 and the educational guidelines for childcare revised three times in 1990, 1999 and 2008, respectively.

In the revision of the course of study for kindergarten in March 1989, the educational content fields became five (health, human relationships, environment, language and expression). Educational guidelines for nursery schools revision followed suit in 1990. Then, in 1998 and 2008 for kindergarten, and in 1999 and 2008 for nursery school, educational standards were revised but these five content fields remained. In 2008 the course of study for kindergarten and an educational guideline for nursery school were revised at the same time. The course of study for the new hybrid educational institution enacted in 2014 carried over the same five educational content fields, which are summarised in Table 7.1.

Critical question

» *How closely does this match the EYFS? Would the training received by a nursery practitioner in England prepare them to work with these aims?*

Table 7.1 *The common educational fields and aims in the course of study for kindergarten and educational guidelines for nursery school*

Fields	Aims
Health	Developing physical and mental health and fostering children's abilities to independently maintain a safe and healthy life. • To act lively and freely and experience a sense of fulfilment. • To fully move the body and to exercise willingly. • To acquire the habits and attitudes necessary for a healthy and safe life.
Human relationships	Developing self-reliance and fostering the ability to communicate with others in order to associate with and support each other. • To enjoy kindergarten life and experience a sense of fulfilment in acting by oneself. • To become familiar with and deepen relationships with others they are close to, and to develop affection and trust. • To acquire socially desirable habits and attitudes.
Environment	Fostering children's abilities to relate to the environment with curiosity and inquisition, and to incorporate this into their daily life. • To develop interest in and curiosity about various kinds of things and experiences around them through a sense of familiarity with their surrounding environment and contact with nature. • To initiate interaction with their surrounding environment, enjoy making and discovering new things and incorporating them into their lives. • To enrich children's understanding of the nature of things, concepts of quantities, written words etc, through observing, thinking about and dealing with surrounding things and experiences.
Language	Developing the will and attitude to verbally express experiences and thoughts in one's own words, as well as to listen to others' spoken words, and fostering an understanding of language and skills of expression. • To experience the enjoyment of expressing personal feelings in their own words. • To listen closely to other people, to verbalise experiences and thoughts, and to enjoy communicating. • To have a grasp of the language necessary for everyday life, to be familiar with picture books and stories, and to communicate feelings with teachers and friends.
Expression	Developing rich feelings and the ability to express oneself, and enhancing creativity by expressing experiences and thoughts in their own words. • To develop a deep sense of the beauty and other qualities of various things. • To enjoy expressing feelings and thoughts in their own way. • To enjoy various ways of self-expression throughout the day using rich imagery.

Critical workforce issues in ECEC in Japan

Gender

Gender imbalance is characteristic of early childhood education workforce and care in Japan. The first kindergarten in Japan was established at Tokyo Women's Teacher College. For a long time, teachers in the childcare had been called 保母 *(Hobo)*; note that one element 母 translates roughly as *mother* in English. In other words, childcare workers were implicitly identified as *women*. Nakamura (2009) pointed out that the purpose of developing nursery schools was to reduce the burden on mothers and to provide a time for household chores. Also, nursery schools were idealised as a place for mother's self-growth through direct consultation and gaining friends (Nakamura, 2009). In the nursery school, the word for practitioners was changed from *Hobo* to *Hoikushi* (保育士 where 士 means certified professionals) in 1997 when the Child Welfare Act was amended.

Currently, there are 544 childcare worker training schools in Japan, admitting the total number of 51,270 students (as of April 2007). The number of students who received a childcare worker certificate was 41,613; 20,238 (72.7 per cent) of them were from junior colleges, 5956 (14.3 per cent) were from universities, and 223 (12.5 per cent) were from vocational schools; 19,124 (46.0 per cent) out of the 41,613 get a job in a nursery school. The junior colleges are major pre-service teacher training institutions for early childhood education in Japan and the majority of junior college students (eg, 88.4 per cent in 2013) are female. This means that the overwhelming majority of nursery workers are women in Japanese nursery schools.

For kindergarten included in the school education system under the School Education Act and the Ministry of Education, Figure 7.1 summarises the ratio of female teachers compared to those in primary schools, secondary schools and high schools from 2003 to 2013.

The flatness of the plots in Figure 7.1 shows that, in the past ten years, there has been no significant change in the proportion of female teachers from kindergarten to high school, and that the percentage of female teachers in kindergartens is very high in comparison with those in primary schools, secondary schools and high schools. In the kindergartens, approximately 93 per cent of teachers are female and this has remained constant for a decade. According to a survey by Kawamata (2008), 70 per cent of kindergarten teachers thought that having a career as a kindergarten teacher is adequate for women and 40 per cent answered that it is good for women to leave a job after giving birth. She noted that there are two stereotypical myths in Japan: the *three-year-old myth* that mothers should devote themselves to nurturing their children up to three years of age and the *maternal myth* that women have a maternal instinct from birth.

Early retirement

As mentioned in the previous section, the majority of young female teachers is a striking characteristic of the workforce of early childhood education in Japan. On the other hand, the workplace is not necessarily considered to be appropriate for women. The high rate of early

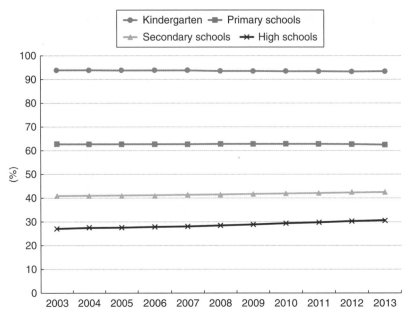

Figure 7.1 *Percentage of female teachers in different school levels from 2003 to 2013*

retirement of teachers from early childhood education could be noted as another notable characteristic of the workforce in Japan.

Table 7.2 summarises the rate of teachers' early retirement in kindergarten, primary schools, secondary school and high school from 2000 to 2012. The table also shows the percentages of male teachers and female teachers in each year per school level. It is clear that the rate of early retirement of teachers in kindergarten is twice higher than those in other school levels, and most of the early retirees are female teachers in kindergarten.

Figure 7.2 shows the average age of early retirees in kindergarten, primary schools, secondary schools and high schools from 2000 to 2012. Regardless of year, younger teachers retired earlier in kindergarten compared to those in primary school, secondary school and high school. The average age of early retirees in kindergarten is about 30 years old; the difference of the average age of early retirees between kindergarten and other school levels is about 20 years. In other words, the high rate of early female teacher retirees should be noted as one of the critical issues in early childhood education and care in Japan.

Kato and Suzuki (2011) reported the early retirees in kindergarten and nursery school gave 'inappropriateness' as the reason for their early retirement. Those in kindergarten answered (1) marriage and (2) health, while those in nursery school reported (1) health and (2) human relationships as reasons for their early retirement. Morimoto, Hayashi and Higashimura (2013) reported that about half of early retirees in kindergarten and nursery schools answered that life events such as marriage, giving birth and child rearing were reasons for their early retirement. In a survey by Okamoto et al (2010), human relationships

Table 7.2 The rate of teachers' early retirement

School year	Kindergarten			Primary schools			Secondary schools			High schools		
2000	3.2	**11.0**	96.8	44.3	**2.3**	55.7	58.0	**2.7**	42.0	76.4	**3.8**	23.6
2003	3.9	**11.1**	96.1	39.3	**3.2**	60.7	58.3	**2.9**	41.7	74.1	**3.8**	25.9
2006	3.9	**11.6**	96.1	38.5	**3.5**	61.5	57.0	**3.0**	43.0	71.1	**3.8**	28.9
2009	4.5	**10.3**	95.5	39.0	**4.0**	61.0	58.4	**3.6**	41.6	71.8	**4.0**	28.2
2012	4.7	**10.6**	95.3	37.1	**4.4**	62.9	59.6	**3.8**	40.4	71.8	**4.4**	28.2

Bold: average retirement rate (% of each sector's workforce per year). Left columns: % male; right columns: % female.

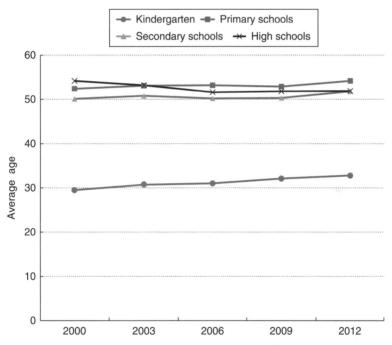

Figure 7.2 Average age of teachers' early retirement in different school levels from 2000 to 2012

and bad health were common reasons for early retirement in kindergarten and nursery school. They also showed differences in the trends of early retirement between public and private kindergarten teachers, with the ratio of early retirees among young teachers in private kindergartens higher than that of young teachers in public kindergartens.

CASE STUDY

Hana

Hana had always wanted to work with little children, ever since she could remember. She liked to play with her young cousins when they visited her family's house in Matsuyama and, when they were older, she organised visits for them to the castle and the gardens. So when it came to thinking about a career, she decided to become a kindergarten teacher. When she left high school, she took a course in Teaching Practice in Kindergarten and was delighted when she managed to get a job at the kindergarten attached to Dogo University. This was an exciting place to teach; her colleagues were full of bright ideas for activities to encourage children's love of nature and understanding of how things worked. Some days she helped children with traditional activities like making dorogango (mudballs) or looking for, catching and caring for insects; other days she encouraged children to explore what was inside every-day machines. She really enjoyed her work, although the days were long and sometimes the work was hard and she felt the stresses and strains of interpersonal relationships in the workplace, but her natural patience and empathy with children meant she always felt in tune with them. Her life got even better when she married her childhood sweetheart Hideo and set up house in the suburbs. Then she found out she was expecting a child – both she and Hideo were overjoyed at the prospect of becoming parents. And after baby Makito was born somehow working in the kindergarten no longer seemed quite as attractive; it didn't seem right anymore. Hana wanted to devote all her time to caring for her own child, so sadly she left her colleagues behind her – although often returned to share with them the excitement of watching and helping Makito to grow strong and inquisitive and sensitive to other people. She was so proud, and caring for her own child was so rewarding – the most important job she could ever have.

Critical questions

» *Which aspects of Hana's story sound familiar to you, and which sound strange or surprising?*

» *What would you like to ask Hana about how she felt on her return visits to the kindergarten?*

Critical reflections

As discussed in this chapter, young women form a big part of the workforce of early childhood education in Japan, but the clear feature of this workforce is its early turnover. In the twenty-first century, views on nurturing children have been changing. The imperative to meet diverse needs of early childhood education, such as extension of daycare and care for sick children, is increasing as the policy targets to meet these diverse needs increase. The rate of poverty among children in Japan is not necessarily low, and regional and income disparities are becoming apparent. The fundamental problem of early childhood education in Japan is how to achieve a compromise between high-quality education and the diverse needs of young children and their families in the twenty-first century.

In Japan, kindergarten is not yet mandated as compulsory education. There is an education standard, as set out in the course of study for kindergarten and educational guidelines for nursery schools, but the power to uphold these standards is weak compared with primary and secondary schools. There is a large difference in turnover of kindergarten teachers and nursery workers between the private and public schools; the working environment, including day-to-day practice, differs greatly between private and public schools and private kindergartens have a particularly high percentage of early turnover. Guidelines for professional development and career planning for private kindergarten and nursery school are required.

From 1639 to 1854, Japan adopted a policy of seclusion. An implicit norm, which is 'education of the Japanese for the Japanese by the Japanese in Japanese' still remains in modern Japanese education (Sumida, 2013b). Learning a foreign language in particular has not been prioritised. In nursery school and kindergarten, the ratio of foreign teachers in nurseries is very low. Although in the twentieth century acceptance of immigrants and foreign workers exists as a national policy, there are very few discussions about how young non-Japanese children and families should be supported in kindergarten or nursery schools. This international book on the workforce of early childhood education and care should prompt useful discussions of Japan's practices and policy in a worldwide context.

Further reading

Holloway, S D (2000) *Contested Childhood: Diversity and Change in Japanese Preschools*. London: Routledge.

Although over a decade old, this book offers a detailed account of the cultural models underpinning Japanese preschools.

Sumida, M (2013) The Japanese View of Nature and Its Implications for the Teaching of Science in the Early Childhood Years, in Georgeson, J and Payler J (eds) *International Perspectives on Early Childhood Education and Care*. Maidenhead: Open University Press, pp 243–56.

Using a detailed case study, this chapter explains how the different way of thinking about nature in Japan shapes how children learn about science.

Oda, Y and Mori, M (2006) Current Challenges of Kindergarten (Yochien) Education in Japan: Toward Balancing Children's Autonomy and Teachers' Intention. *Childhood Education*, 82(6): 369–73.

Taking an historical overview, this article responds to criticism that kindergarten overemphasises free play and encourages children to become self-centred and disruptive when they start school.

References

Kato, M and Suzuki, K (2011) Study on Early Turnover of New Teachers at Child Welfare Facilities. *Bulletin of Tokiwa University Junior College*, 42: 79–94. (in Japanese)

Kawamata, M (2008) A Study on the Life Course of Pre-school Teachers: Gender Role Attitudes of Pre-school Teachers and Students in Colleges of Early Childhood Education. *Bulletin of Fukuoka Woman's Junior College*, 71: 17–26. (in Japanese)

Kuraray (2014) Research Report on What Grade 1 Children Want to Be in the Future. [online] Available at: www.kuraray.co.jp/enquete/occupation/ (accessed 5 December 2014) (in Japanese)

Morimoto, M, Hayashi, Y and Higashimura, T (2013) A Survey on Newcomer Child-care Workers' Early Retirement. *Bulletin of Narabunka Women's College*, 44: 101–9. (in Japanese)

My navi news (2013) [online] Available at: woman.mynavi.jp/article/130225-010/ (accessed 10 December 2014) (in Japanese)

Nakamura, T (2009). *The Development of Early Childhood Education Policy after World War II and its Future.* Tokyo: Shindokusyo Sha. (in Japanese)

Ogawa, C (2013) Early Turnover at Kindergarten and Child Welfare Facilities – Based on Trend Surveys and the Current Situation of Graduates. *Bulletin of the School of Social Work Seirei Christopher University*, 11: 55–64. (in Japanese)

Okamoto, K, Shimeda, S, Matsui, R and Kitano, K (2010) Present Situations and Problems of Early Resignation from Kindergartens and Nursery Schools. *Bulletin of Tokiwakai College Early Childhood Education*, 39: 19–39. (in Japanese)

Sakamoto, H (2008) *Sozo Kurahashi: The Man and Ideas*. Froebel Kan. (in Japanese)

Sumida, M (2013a) The Japanese View of Nature and Its Implications for the Teaching of Science in the Early Childhood Years, in Georgeson, J and Payler J (eds) *International Perspectives on Early Childhood Education and Care*. Maidenhead: Open University Press, pp 243–56.

Sumida, M (2013b) Book Reviews: International Education Policy in Japan in an Age of Globalisation and Risk. *Journal of Education for Teaching*, 39(4): 467–79.

Suwa, Y (2007) *The Japanese Idea of Early Childhood Education and Sozo Kurahashi*. Shindokusyosya. (in Japanese)

The Editorial Committee of Child Care Workers Training (ed) (2007) *The Principle of Child Care*. National Council of Social Welfare. (in Japanese)

The New Editorial Committee of Child Care Workers Training (ed) (2014) *The Principle of Child Care*. National Council of Social Welfare. (in Japanese)

Part C
Political histories

8 Germany: parallel histories in ECEC

ULRIKE HOHMANN

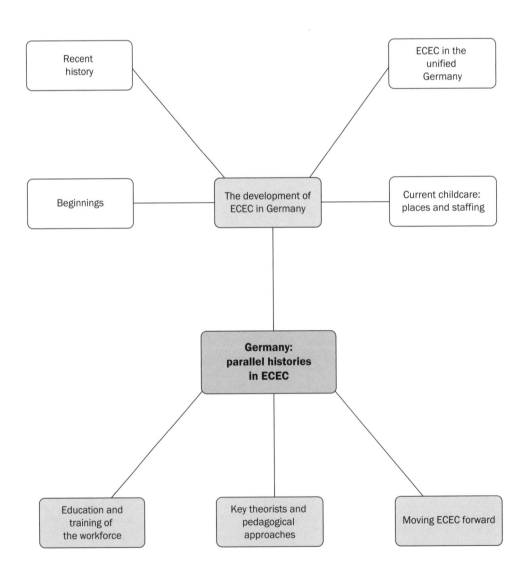

Introduction

Germany is a federal state consisting of 16 regions (*Bundesländer*) with regional governments. In 1990, the socialist German Democratic Republic (East Germany) and the Federal Republic of Germany (West Germany), which had been established in the aftermath of World War II, were reunified. About a quarter century later, socio-economic and cultural differences between the former Federal Germany and the new *Länder* continue to exist and are particularly prominent in relation to childcare.

In 2012 about 82 million people lived in Germany, with around 16 per cent of these in the new *Länder*. Twenty per cent of the German inhabitants have a migration background, that is, they were born in another country or have at least one parent who was born in another country. Overall there were about 3.3 million children under the age of six. They made up 4 per cent of the population and 33 per cent of these children have a migration background. Most of these children and their families live in the Western *Länder* (Statistisches Bundesamt, 2013c).

Childcare services are part of child and youth welfare sector. Essential legislation is provided by basic law and the 1990 Children and Youth Assistant Act, which states the basic rights of children and families and delegates further regulations to the 16 *Länder* including the duty to organise, control and finance child and youth welfare services. ECEC services, like other welfare provision, are bound by the principles of subsidiarity. Foremost the family is responsible for the well-being of its members. Services that cannot be provided by the family, like childcare, should be provided by free providers (so-called because they can choose to stop provision) and public services are only established if non-governmental organisations (NGOs) are unable to do so. These not-for-profit NGOs receive money from the *Land*, the municipality and fees from parents to provide childcare independently. About a third are public providers, another third affiliated to the Protestant or Catholic church, others include associations following a particular pedagogical approach and parent associations. Only about 2 per cent are for-profit providers (Statistisches Bundesamt, 2013a).

The development of ECEC in Germany

Beginnings

The first institutions for children emerged at the beginning of the nineteenth century in Germany in the context of industrialisation. *Kleinkinderbewahranstalten* (literally translated: infant shelter institutions) aimed to keep poor working-class children off the streets and protect them from accidents or slipping into criminality. Many of these institutions were initiated and/or overseen by middle-class women under the umbrella of philanthropy. They offered practical solutions to working parents but also pursuits to instil work-related skills and ethics and some middle-class values. The necessity to educate the poor was widely discussed and seen as an opportunity to keep social unrest at bay. *Kleinkinderschulen* (infant schools) set up by the church, for example by the Protestant theologian Theodor Fliedner (1800–60), served the same purpose along with the religiously justified salvation of children's souls. Charity became in times of social change a new missionary tool (Erning, 1987).

CASE STUDY

Fröbel's kindergarten

Friedrich Fröbel (1782–1852) distanced himself from targeting unsupervised or neglected children and called his vision of learning opportunities for all children *Kindergarten*. Children had opportunities to attend the garden, play active games as a group and to play with *Gaben* (gifts), educational toys that Fröbel had developed. Kindergarten offered supplementary, not replacement, care and education for children in families, and aimed to support and educate mothers in their task of raising children. His kindergarten pedagogy should be seen as part of his understanding of *Bildung* (education) and the institutional structures he had set up, including a school, education for parents and training the workforce. Fröbel saw children as active learners in need of guidance to move from the sensual to the abstract. Starting points are day-to-day activities and the natural context like the village and the family home where children grow up. Engagement with Fröbel's gifts would enable young children to understand structures (Heiland, 2010). Fröbel's pedagogical and educational ideas were welcomed by the bourgeois middle classes and by those avoiding childcare institutions affiliated to the church. The Prussian monarchy feared damaging influences on the status quo, undermining the ideal of the family with its gendered roles, and consequently prohibited Fröbel kindergartens between 1851 and 1860.

Critical question

»   *How closely does Fröbel's vision match the EYFS? Do mothers (and fathers) still need educating to raise children – and if so, whose job should this be?*

Division between kindergartens for middle-class children and working-class children continued throughout the nineteenth century. The prominence of the ideal of the patriarchal bourgeois family, with a caring housewife and a strong, essential bond between mother and child, reserved public education and care for young children for families in need, regulated by the Prussian Statute on Youth Welfare Education 1890.

At the beginning of the twentieth century other child-centred approaches gained acceptance and kindergartens adopting principles introduced by Maria Montessori (1870–1952) or Rudolf Steiner (1861–1925) were established. After World War I and the abolition of the monarchy, Social Democrats and other parties on the left promoted a unified education system comprising all institutions from kindergarten to university. However, there was strong resistance from churches and the Fröbel Association. Childcare remained part of the welfare sector and attending kindergarten remained voluntary. The Imperial Youth Welfare Act 1922 introduced the subsidiarity principle, which declares private providers (at the time mainly protestant and catholic churches) to be the main providers and only allows and obliges municipalities to step in if private provision was insufficient. This organising principle is still in place (Scheiwe, 2009).

Under Hitler's fascism (1933–45) attempts to subsume all kindergartens under the control of the National Socialist People's Welfare were not entirely successful despite the closure of private kindergartens and the ban on welfare associations linked to trade unions. Both churches were able to maintain responsibility for kindergartens which accommodated practices to promote health and physical fitness, strict gender roles, racist ideology and the glorification of Hitler (Berger, 1986).

Recent history

After 1945 childcare provision in the two emerging German states, the German Democratic Republic (a socialist state) and the Federal Republic of Germany, went different ways. Both states had to find ways to distance themselves from the family and childcare policies of Nazism. The socialist East Germany aimed to break with older German social and family policy traditions and West Germany picked up ideals from before 1933, the onset of fascism. At the same time West Germany strove to distance herself from the new policies made in GDR (Bast and Ostner, 1992). East Germany invested heavily in full-time childcare, free to parents apart from a small fee towards meals. Childcare facilities for children from the age of three became part of the education system. Care for younger children was the responsibility of the health ministry (Boeckmann, 1993). For both age groups clear frameworks and practice guidance were developed centrally (Beu et al, 1971). By 1990, just before the reunification of Germany, there were places for 95 per cent of the 3–6-year-old children and 80 per cent of children under the age of three in East Germany (Statistisches Amt der DDR, 1990). Most parents appreciated the contribution childcare settings made to the care and education of their children (Winkel, Kerkhoff and Machalowski, 1995).

West German welfare policy relied on ideals of the traditional male breadwinner family. From this perspective there was no need for full-time childcare. The family and motherly care were seen as the best environment for young children. Attending childcare settings was perceived to be harmful to children below the age of three, as was full-time care for older children. Working mothers relied on childcare by grandmothers or family daycare providers. Childcare in the private homes of childminders was seen as closest to the ideal of motherly care (BMFSF, 1996). From their third birthday children might benefit from attending part-time kindergarten promoting socialisation with other children and development of school readiness. Kindergartens were the responsibility of the Youth Office and, true to the subsidiarity principle, 80 per cent of the part-time places were provided by the two main churches (Tietze, 1993). Up until the 1970s there were places for around a third of children aged 3–6, mostly part-time, and for less than one per cent of younger children. Places for 3–6-year-old children were increased in reaction to the launch of Sputnik, but not for younger children (see Tietze, 1993). Kindergartens were declared as the first rung of the education system but remained the responsibility of the Youth Office. By 1990 there were places for just under 70 per cent of 3–6 years olds, with only 15 per cent offering full-time care, and for just under two per cent of younger children, although with a higher proportion of full-time provision. Parents had to pay for childcare, albeit subsidised by municipalities and *Land*, and costs were kept relatively low because providers were not-for-profit organisations.

Critical questions

» *How could the launch of the Sputnik satellite by Russia shape educational planning in other countries?*

» *Can you identify an event in another country shaping current educational policy?*

ECEC in the unified Germany

The past 25 years show a number of influences on the ECEC landscape, some accelerated by reunification. Demographic changes like the decreasing fertility rate, the aging population and effects of immigration fuel calls for restructuring the education system, as do attitudinal changes towards childhood and gendered interpretations of work–life balance. The importance attached to each of the two driving perspectives on ECEC – as services to free parents to engage in paid work and as important educational institutions – has changed and their scope has extended.

The new Child and Assistance Act 1990 of the reunified Germany incorporated early years services of the new *Länder* into the West German system. The combination of socio-economic, demographic and welfare policy changes led to a rapid cutback of places and closure of daycare facilities. After rejecting a more liberal approach to abortion rights and to affirm the state's interest in children's well-being, the new Act, as a compromise between the two systems, set out a legal entitlement from 1996 to a place in kindergarten or family daycare for three-year-old children until enrolment in school (Scheiwe, 2009). However, the entitlement covers only a part-time place and parents have to pay fees.

The next impetus for change arose from a particular combination of demographic conditions and shifts in attitudes towards families and children. Demographic changes, which affect social cohesion or place greater financial responsibilities on the shoulders of younger people to provide for a larger proportion of elderly people, highlight the importance of ECEC in the education of the future workforce. As women became less willing to take up the traditional role of housewife and mother, the more equal division of work and caring commitments between partners increases the demand for childcare with longer opening hours.

In this context the findings of the newly established Programme for International Student Assessment (PISA) of 15-year-old students, published in 2001, hit a raw nerve. The results were unexpectedly negative. Germany was ranked in the middle ground with a huge range of abilities, high proportion of 'risk' students with very low competencies, wide gaps between social classes and in particular the negative impact of migration background. Instant reactions included aims to improve children's language competencies, closer co-operation between preschool and primary school, support for disadvantaged children, introduction and monitoring of standards with language tests and programmes (Klieme et al, 2010).

Attention turned to reform of early years education as a lever to improve children's outcomes. All *Länder* began to formulate frameworks and guidance to promote quality, by stating and exemplifying the duty of early childhood settings to provide care and education, working together with parents and documenting learning processes. The task is to extend the definition of *Bildung* in the sense of a comprehensive, continuous improvement of the individual's capacity to act, aiming towards a self-determined life (BMFSFJ, 2013, p 50). Particular efforts have to be made to support children disadvantaged by disability or structural conditions. Structural risks impact cumulatively on children's opportunities to achieve; growing up in a family where parents are educationally disadvantaged, in a household socially or financially at risk puts children under strain. Although the proportion of children in all of these risk constellations is decreasing there are still 12 per cent of children growing up in a family where parents have low educational levels, 10 per cent of children grow up in a household socially disadvantaged through unemployment and 18 per cent of children grow up in a household where the income is below 60 per cent of the median income. Twenty-nine per cent of children are found in one of these risk groups and there are three per cent of children who are affected by all three risks. Children growing up in single parent families with a migration background, especially from Turkish origins, are disproportionately represented (Autorengruppe Bildungsberichterstattung, 2012).

Discussion regarding when support for disadvantaged children is most effective informed the Child Promotion Act 2009 providing legal entitlement to a place when a child reaches her first birthday from August 2013. Strategies to fulfil this obligation included establishing new settings, existing providers increasing their places and some traditional kindergarten offering places to two year olds. Eastern *Länder* are in a better position because they can fall back on existing infrastructures and purpose-built accommodation.

Current childcare: places and staffing

The Barcelona targets, providing places for 90 per cent of 3–6 year old children, have been met in all *Länder*. The target to establish places for 33 per cent of under 3 year olds has still not been met in Germany, although the Eastern *Länder* do (Statistische Ämter des Bundes und der Länder, 2013; European Commission, 2014).

By 31 March 2013 there were about 2.5 million children aged six or under attending a daycare setting or a family daycarer. Of those 596,300 were under three years old. Around 15 per cent are looked after by a family daycarer. However, these children are usually under the age of three. The proportion of children 3–6 years of age in family daycare is small at 0.6 per cent. However, there were 13,100 children who stayed with a family daycare provider in addition to attending other forms of daycare (Statistische Ämter des Bundes und der Länder, 2013). Daycare for children 3–6 is well accepted and 93 per cent visit a kindergarten. The uptake of places for younger children is 29.3 per cent on average, though for Eastern *Länder* including Berlin the rate was 49.8 per cent compared with 24.2 per cent in Western parts of Germany (Statistisches Bundesamt, 2013b). Children in Eastern parts are more likely to attend childcare and more likely to stay full-time (Autorengruppe Bildungsberichterstattung, 2014).

At 31 March there were 52,486 settings of various sizes registered, with 496,299 employees (practitioners, heads and administration). Most of the practitioners are *Erzieherinnen* (70 per cent), followed by *Kinderpflegerinnen* (12 per cent) but only 0.3 per cent of *Kindheitspädagoginnen*. Only 5 per cent of the workforce is male and they tend to work in leadership positions or with older children. Most practitioners have contracts between 21 to 38 hours per week. Full-time employment is available to only a third and 17 per cent are employed on contracts below 21 hours (Statistisches Bundesamt, 2013a). Another concern is the ageing of practitioners and the pressure to increase training of new staff (Autorengruppe Bildungsberichterstattung, 2012).

Education and training of the workforce

Parallel to the development of daycare facilities outlined above, the preparation, training and education of staff mirrored changing perceptions of childhood and adults' responsibilities for children's care and education. At the beginning of the nineteenth century women were prepared by more experienced staff. The protestant theologian Theodor Fliedner began to train infant teachers in 1836, Friedrich Fröbel prepared *Kindergärtnerinnen* to work in the kindergarten and there was also preparation to work with children in Catholic institutions. Over time these main training providers established courses; many became integrated into women's colleges and developed common training standards. The occupations *Kindergärtnerin* as well as *Jugendleiterin* (youth leader) were established and state-approved. By the end of the Weimar Republic, further specialisms in work with school-aged children and work in residential homes had been added (Amthor, 2003). The pedagogical approach to work in kindergartens was based on Fröbel, though reform pedagogy, such as Montessori methods, influenced the training of *Kindergartnerinnen*. *Kinderpflegerinnen* were trained to care for babies and very young children, often in families.

After World War II, training structures and occupations returned to the systems before Nazism. Increasing interest in preschool education and its potential to address disadvantage and the wider educational debate following the Sputnik shock led in 1967 to the new occupation *Staatlich Anerkannte Erzieherin* (state-approved educator) trained to work in all kinds of childhood institutions with children of all ages, but not as teachers in schools. Training is offered in post-secondary, vocational colleges or academies with a focus on social pedagogy. Admission initially required a year-long work placement and but now requires a qualification in the field or in another occupation. The training generally comprises two years at college followed by a one-year internship. The occupation *Kinderpflegerin* continues (though now replaced in some *Länder* with *Sozialassistentin*); it requires lower entry qualification, the training is shorter and prepares for work alongside *Erzieherinnen*. Additionally the role of *Jugendleiterinnen* was replaced with training as *Sozialpädagoge*, equipping practitioners to lead institutions concerned with social welfare, support social pedagogical engagement and work with individuals. Women who had qualified in one of the East German occupations had to retrain or take part in continuous professional development to cover all areas of the broader occupation *Erzieherin* as established in West Germany.

Discussions to reform training and education of the early years workforce were rekindled by the emphasis on early education as an answer to PISA 2000 results and with it the changing role of *Erzieherinnen*, the requirements of the Bologna process to standardise training and education, and comparison of qualification levels with other countries. The first BA and MA courses were established in 2004. Concerns were raised about the feasibility of introducing new roles with higher income expectations (Pasternack and Schildberg, 2005), the role these newly qualified people would take up in ECEC institutions (Thole and Cloos, 2006), the skills and competencies needed to work in ECEC and whether universities were able to support students in gaining these (Diller and Rauschenbach, 2006). It was feared that lifting the education and training of the workforce onto higher education level would lead to the disappearance of vocational training colleges (*Fachschule*) and consequently undermine training opportunities for the traditional pool of young people (Thole and Cloos, 2006).

Since training first moved to universities, agreement has been reached to position courses at *Fachschule* at the same level as BA courses at universities of applied science or other universities, which also allows credits awarded in one institution to count towards awards studied in another (KMK und JFMK, 2010). Ten years on, WIFF (2014) lists 95 Bachelor's and 19 Master's courses. These courses vary in their location, teaching and learning mode, entrance qualification, titles and final awards. Even the title of occupation is not agreed upon. Some are called *Kindheitspädagogen* (childhood pedagogues), others *Frühpädagogen* (literally: early pedagogues) (Dreyer, 2010). It is not clear whether these courses lead to a distinctive occupation with different skills and competencies. However, comparison of child-related and environment-related competencies does not show any significant differences between people who had trained either at *Fachschule* or university (Mischo, 2014). It remains to be seen how *Kindheitspädagoginnen* integrate into the ECEC landscape, whether the qualification enables them to achieve higher incomes. There are concerns that those with higher education awards will choose to work in areas other than ECEC (Fuchs-Rechlin, 2013), and that employers lack information about the qualification, so *Kindheitspädagoginnen* often work under the same conditions and with the same pay as *Erzieherinnen* (Kirstein and Fröhlich-Gildhoff, 2014).

Critical questions

» *How do you think salary levels for the early years workforce should be decided?*

» *What are the barriers to basing salary levels on qualifications?*

Key theorists and pedagogical approaches

The ethos of kindergartens and other forms of childcare provision can still be linked to Fröbel's emphasis on the child as active learner, the benefits of playing in a group with other children and the importance of playing outside. Most of Fröbel's gifts may have disappeared from mainstream kindergartens, although the set of wooden blocks remains a staple toy in kindergartens. Group games using music and movement to engage with children, the closeness to nature and changes through the seasons and the view of the child as active learner benefitting from a meaningful and everyday life environment are the legacy of Fröbel.

Any textbook for *Erzieherinnen* contains descriptions of other pedagogical approaches to working with young children. Readers are introduced to the classics, Montessori and Steiner, as well as to Freinet, Reggio Emilia and the situational approach. Often approaches are just described but differences are not discussed. This alerts students to a variety of future roles and serves as an invitation to explore further, but it may be difficult to develop a professional identity. Although perspectives may cover common ground, details may be contradictory. Structural quality, for example the age and group structure established in a setting, can affect process quality, that is, didactics (as teaching and learning is called in Germany). How does the *Erzieherin* relate to a child, what role does she take in children's play and what are the expectations between staff and parents? It is not surprising that there is no didactics of early years (Kasüschke, 2010).

The history of early childcare and the political context of establishing plurality by making *Länder* responsible for education as a bulwark against totalitarian developments explains to some extent why there is no agreement on pedagogical or didactical approaches in early years. Additionally the double motivation inherent in ECEC provision to release parents into the labour market and to educate children, and a changing balance in the German context, add to the sector's insecurities; strong elements of care, especially for young children, exist alongside acknowledgement of the potential for education although perhaps more as socialisation. The inclusion of even younger children and the extension from part-time to full-time daily attendance in settings means physical care aspects must be considered too. When pre-school education and methods were introduced in the 70s, requirements were too abstract and too demanding and they soon slipped back into 'simple theory of practice' (Retter 1983 in Roux, 2002). Soft, holistic pedagogy settled in kindergartens and influenced practices in primary school. A number of pedagogical approaches developed which we still find listed in textbooks for *Erzieherinnen*.

The second wave of ECEC reforms resulted in a general framework for ECEC and more specific frameworks in each of the *Länder*. Some are presented as guidance, others as compulsory. Each of these will be adapted to the particular ideological stance of individual institutions. For example settings established by the church will include Christian principles. The training and education of staff require knowledge of different pedagogical models, including the classics (Fröbel, Montessori, Steiner), to more recent forms of reform pedagogy (Reggio Emilia, Freinet and situation-oriented work) and approaches embedded in particular structures, like forest kindergarten, settings without fixed groups or bilingual settings – and textbooks for *Erzieherinnen* and *Kindheitspädagoginnen* contain information on most of them (Böcher et al, 2010; Jaszus et al, 2008; Knauf, Düx and Schlüter, 2007). There is no agreement on what a successful way of working with children and their families looks like (Kasüschke, 2010). A comparison of underlying assumptions and beliefs about the nature of children and adults, ideals and methods is necessary. However, there is agreement on the necessity to have a clear vision and approach, which needs to be developed within a setting and with parents to be communicated to the community.

Critical question

» *Is is possible to study different pedagogical models and then enact whichever is in place in a setting, or can you only work with an approach that you believe in? Explain your answer as fully as possible.*

Moving ECEC forward

In order to move the development of early years education forward, Roux suggests exploring different approaches to Bildung (education) as, for example, discussed by Klafki (1978 in Roux, 2002): material education with a focus on content and the aim to develop a canon of knowledge that children and young people acquire in order to open up the world. It evokes the image of the child as *tabula rasa* and poses difficulties in deciding what should be included. Nevertheless, adults do have ideas about what they think children should learn; any kind of curriculum, curriculum guidance or textbooks for practitioners will express preferences for a specific kind of core content.

Formal education aims to open up the individual to the world. If education is understood as process, however, in the sense of developing competencies or skills for learning, it is less obvious how adults can support children in doing so. Children are expected to develop the ability to reflect, become independent, to gain command of methods and to deal with conflicts. This perspective neglects content. Here the discourse of the child as competent learner, taken to its extreme, renders adults superfluous or reduces their role to that of environment preparer.

Material and formal education are two sides of the same coin. What deserves attention are processes and how adults relate to children. The Children and Youth Assistant Act 1990 states the right of the child to *Betreuung* (a combination of care and supervision), *Bildung* (education) and *Erziehung* (socialisation, enculturation of the child to introduce her to the adult world) but does not qualify further how early childhood education and care settings contribute to these. Approaching the education of young children interchangeably with socialisation and an emphasis on relational aspects opens up opportunities for enjoyment of activities that promote education and co-construction of knowledge. For example, children and adults sharing picture books will have access to all aspects: *Betreuung, Bildung* and *Erziehung.*

Critical reflections

This chapter has traced the parallel developments in ECEC provision and workforce in Germany, showing how these have been shaped by political changes and underlying theoretical concepts.

It might lead you to think about your own understanding of Bildung and reflect on what and how much knowledge must be acquired in order to qualify as being educated or, in relation to early years, as being school ready, and whether that is the aim of early years provision.

The German development highlights the different purposes of ECEC. Do you feel ECEC should focus on freeing parents' time and releasing them from some care and education duties or do you prefer to think about ECEC as educating children? In what kind of setting would you prefer to work and what concepts of families, children and education system would that require?

Further reading

Hohmann, U (under review) From Kindergarten to Early Childhood Education and Care in Germany: New Demands on the Workforce. *Professional Development in Education.*

In this article I use the concepts *Erziehung, Bildung* and *Betreuung* (roughly enculturation, education and care) to analyse the structural development and perceptions of ECE and what this means for the workforce.

May, H (2013) *The Discovery of Early Childhood* (2nd edn). Wellington: NZCER Press.

Chapter 4 Froebel Kindergartens: "The Plays of Childhood" is a good introduction to Fröbel and includes pictures and images which help to get a good feel for this approach.

Scheiwe, K (2009) Slow Motion – Institutional Factors as Obstacles to the Expansion of Early Childhood Education in the FRG, in Scheiwe, K and Willenkens, H (eds) *Child Care and Preschool Development in Europe: Institutional Perspectives*. Basingstoke: Palgrave Macmillan.

This chapter explains the developments in Germany in more depth.

References

Amthor, R-C (2003) *Die Geschichte der Berufsausbildung in der Sozialen Arbeit: Auf der Suche nach Professionalisierung und Identität*. Weinheim: Juventa.

Autorengruppe Bildungsberichterstattung (2012) *Bildung in Deutschland 2012: Ein indikatorengestützter Bericht mit einer Analyse zur kulturellen Bildung im Lebenslauf*. Bielefeld: Bertelsmann.

Autorengruppe Bildungsberichterstattung (2014) *Bildung in Deutschland 2012: Ein indikatorengestützter Bericht mit einer Analyse zur Bildung von Menschen mit Behinderungen*. Bielefeld: Bertelsmann.

Bast, K and Ostner, I (1992) Ehe und Familie in der Sozialpolitik der DDR und BRD – ein Vergleich, in Schmähl, W (ed) ZfSU *Sozialpolitik im Prozeß der deutschen Vereinigung*. Frankfurt, New York: Campus.

Berger, M (1986) *Vorschulerziehung im Nationalsozialismus: Recherchen zur Situation des Kindergartenwesens 1933–1945*. Weinheim: Beltz.

Beu, W, Dumke, I, Freese, I, Jürgens, A, Krase, E, Michaelis, H, Michaelis, S, Müller, L, Rösler, J and Rosenbaum, U (eds) (1971) *Pädagogische Studientexte zur Vorschulerziehung*. Berlin: Volk und Wissen, Volkseigener Verlag.

Böcher, H, Ellinghaus, B, König, E, Langenmayr, M, Österreicher, H, Rödel, B, Schleth-Tams, E, ter Haar, C and Wagner, Y (2010) *Erziehen, bilden und begleiten: Das Lehrbuch für Erzieherinnen und Erzieher*. Troisdorf: Bildungsverlag EINS.

Boeckmann, B (1993) Das Früherziehungssystem in der ehemaligen DDR, in Tietze, W and Roßbach, H-G (eds) *Erfahrungsfelder in der frühen Kindheit: Bestandsaufnahme, Perspektiven*. Freiburg im Breisgau: Lambertus.

Bundesministerium für Familie Senioren Frauen und Jugend (ed) (1996) *Kinderbetreuung in Tagespflege: Tagesmütter-Handbuch*. Stuttgart, Berlin, Köln: Kohlhammer.

Bundesministerium für Familie Senioren Frauen und Jugend (2013) *Vierzehnter Kinder- und Jugendbericht: Bericht über die Lebenssituation von jungen Menschen und die Leistungen der Kinder- und Jugendhilfe in Deutschland*. BMFSFJ Bonn: Bundestagsdrucksache.

Diller, A and Rauschenbach, T (eds) (2006) *Reform oder Ende der Erzieherinnenausbildung? Beiträge zu einer kontroversen Fachdebatte*. München: DJI Verlag Deutsches Jugendinstitut.

Dreyer, R (2010) Kindheitspädagogin versus Erzieherin: Klassische und neue Akteure im Feld der Kindertagesbetreuung. *Theory und Praxis der Sozialpädagogik*, 5, 12–16.

Erning, G (1987) Geschichte der öffentlichen Kleinkinderziehung von den Anfängen bis zum Kaiserreich, in Erning, G, Neumann, K and Reyer, J (eds) *Geschichte des Kindergartens. Band I: Entstehung und Entwicklung der öffentlichen Kleinkindererziehung in Deutschland von den Anfängen bis zur Gegenwart.* Freiburg: Lampertus.

European Commission (2014) *Use of Childcare Services in the EU Member States and Progress Towards the Barcelona Targets: Short Statistical Report No. 1.* Brussel: RAND.

Fuchs-Rechlin, K (2013) *Übergang von fachschul- und hochschulausgebildeten pädagogischen Fachkräften in den Arbeitsmarkt: Erste Befunde der Absolventenbefragung 2012.* Dortmund, Landau, Frankfurt: Projektgruppe ÜFA.

Heiland, H (2010) Fröbels Pädagogik der Kindheit – didaktische Überlegungen zu seiner Spielpädagogik, in Kasüschke, D (ed) *Didaktik in der Pädagogik der frühen Kindheit.* Kronach: Carl Link.

Jaszus, R, Büchin-Wilhelm, I, Mäder-Berg, M and Gutmann, W (2008) *Sozialpädagogische Lernfelder für Erzieherinnen.* Stuttgart: Holland + Josenhans Verlag.

Kasüschke, D (ed) (2010) *Didaktik in der Pädagogik der frühen Kindheit.* Köln Kronach: Carl Link.

Kirstein, N and Fröhlich-Gildhoff, K (2014) Wie stehen die Kita-Träger in Baden-Württemberg zu den Absolventinnen der BA Kindheitspädagogik-Studiengänge?. *Frühe Bildung*, 3(1): 52–4.

Klieme, E, Jude, N, Baumert, J and Prenzel, M (2010) PISA 2000–2009: Bilanz der Veränderung im Schulsystem, in Klieme, E, Artelt, C, Hartig, J, Jude, N, Köller, O, Prenzel, M, Schneider, W and Stanat, P (eds) *PISA 2009.* Münster: Waxmann.

KMK und JFMK (2010) Weiterentwicklung der Aus-, Fort- und Weiterbildung von Erzieherinnen und Erziehern. [online] Available at: www.kmk.org/fileadmin/veroeffentlichunen_beschluesse/2010/2010_09_16-Ausbildung-Erzieher-KMK-JFMK.pdf [online] (accessed 31 May 2014).

Knauf, T, Düx, G and Schlüter, D (2007) *Handbuch Pädagogischer Ansätze: Praxisorientierte Konzpetions- und Qualitätsentwicklung in Kindertageseinrichtungen.* Berlin, Düsseldorf, Mannheim: Cornelsen Verlag Scriptor.

Mischo, C (2014) Early Childhood Teachers' Perceived Competence During Transition from Teacher Education to Work: Results from a Longitudinal Study. *Professional Development in Education*, online, 21 pp.

Pasternack, P and Schildberg, A (2005) Die finanzielle Auswirkung einer Akademisierung der ErzieherInnen-Ausbildung, in Sachverständigenkommission Zwölfter Kinder- und Jugendbericht (ed) *Entwicklungspotenziale institutioneller Angebote im Elementarbereich: Materialien zum Zwölften Kinder- und Jugendbericht, Band 2.* München: Deutsches Jugendinstitut.

Roux, S (2002) PISA und die Folgen: Der Kindergarten zwischen Bildungskatastrophe und Bildungseuphorie. [online] Available at: www.kindergartenpaedagogik.de/967.html (accessed 27 November 2014).

Scheiwe, K (2009) Slow Motion – Institutional Factors as Obstacles to the Expansion of Early Childhood Education in the FRG, in Scheiwe, K and Willenkens, H (eds) *Child Care and Preschool Development in Europe: Institutional Perspectives.* Basingstoke: Palgrave Macmillan.

Statistische Ämter des Bundes und der Länder (2013) *Kindertagesbetreuung 2013 regional: Ein Vergleich aller 402 Kreise in Deutschland.* Wiesbaden: Statistisches Bundesamt.

Statistisches Amt der DDR (1990) *Statistisches Jahrbuch der Deutschen Demokratischen Republik.* Berlin: Statistisches Amt der DDR.

Statistisches Bundesamt (2013a) *Statistiken der Kinder- und Jugendhilfe: Kinder und tätige Personen in Tageseinrichtungen und in öffentlich geförderter Kindertagespflege am 01.03.2013.* Wiesbaden: Statistisches Bundesamt.

Statistisches Bundesamt (2013b) Pressemitteilung 315/13: 29,3% der unter 3-Jährigen am 1. März 2013 in Kindertagesbetreuung. destatis. [online] Available at: https://www.destatis.de/DE/PresseService/Presse/Pressemitteilungen/2013/09/PD13_315_225pdf.pdf?__blob=publicationFile (accessed 25 May 2014).

Statistisches Bundesamt (2013c) *Bevölkerung und Erwerbstätigkeit: Bevölkerung mit Migrationshintergrund: Ergebnisse des Mikrozensus 2012.* Wiesbaden: Statistisches Bundesamt. [online] Available at: www.destatis.de/DE/Publikationen/Thematisch/Bevoelkerung/MigrationIntegration/Migrationshintergrund2010220127004.pdf?__blob=publicationFile (accessed 27 November 2014).

Thole, W and Cloos, P (2006) Akademisierung des Personals für das Handlungsfeld Pädagogik der Kindheit, in Diller, A and Rauschenbach, T (eds) *Reform oder Ende der Erzieherinnenausbildung? Beiträge zu einer kontroversen Fachdebatte.* München: DJI Verlag Deutsches Jugendinstitut.

Tietze, W (1993) Institutionelle Erfahrungsfelder für Kinder im Vorschulalter: Zur Entwicklung vorschulischer Erziehung in Deutschland, in Tietze, W and Roßbach, H-G (eds) *Erfahrungsfelder in der frühen Kindheit: Bestandsaufnahme, Perspektiven.* Freiburg im Breisgau: Lambertus.

Weiterbildungsinitiative Frühpädagogische Fachkräfte (2014) Studiengansdatenbank. [online] Available at: www.weiterbildungsinitiative.de/studium-und-weiterbildung/studium/studiengangsdatenbank/ (accessed 26 May 2014).

Winkel, R, Kerkhoff, E and Machalowski, G (1995) *Zur Lage junger erwerbstätiger Mütter in den neuen Bundesländern, insbesondere zur Wirksamkeit von Erziehungsurlaub und Erziehungsgeld.* ed. Bundesministerium für Familie, S, Frauen und Jugend, Schriftenreihe. vol. 100. Stuttgart, Berlin, Köln: Kohlhammer.

9 Hungarian perspectives on early years workforce development

ANIKÓ NAGY VARGA, BALÁZS MOLNÁR, SÁNDOR PÁLFI AND SÁNDOR SZEREPI

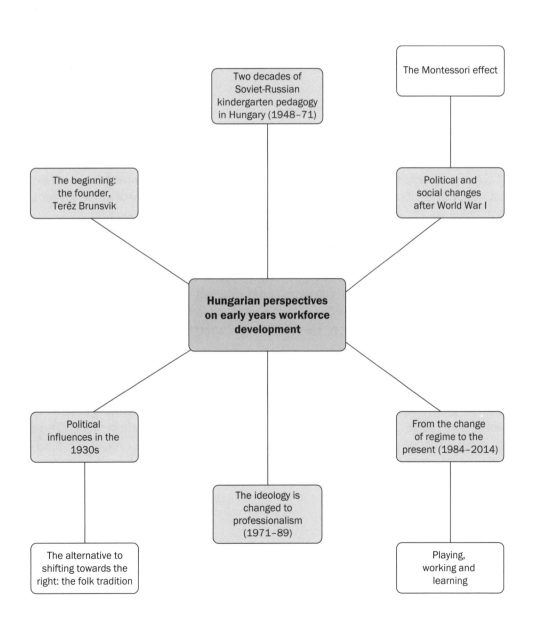

The beginning: the founder, Teréz Brunszvik

Kindergartens as we know them today are the result of historical, political and theoretical developments. In Hungary the role of early education has been characterised by the civilian process. The history of Hungarian kindergartens started with the publication of Samuel Wilderspin's Infant Education in 1825. Wilderspin gained credit in Europe for spreading approaches for working in kindergartens, despite his use of methods applied in schools. The first kindergarten opened in Hungary in 1828, founded by Teréz Brunszvik, was the first institution of this kind in Central Europe. The development of the pedagogical nature of the first kindergartens was deeply influenced by the English approaches as Brunszvik was influenced by the work of Wilderspin (Pukánszky, 2005). Later, more infant schools were established. In 1836, the Infant School Propagator Society of Hungary was founded resulting in an increase in the number of infant schools in the country. The primary goal of the society was to organise and maintain infant schools, consider the intellectual education of children and train educators. The first infant schools were independent; they did not belong to the school districts supervising public schools.

It is important to establish that in the time of Brunszvik we cannot refer to kindergartens as we know them today, hence our use of infant schools. The historical context meant children were educated based on the principles of didactics found at the primary education level. From Brunszvik's notes we can get an insight of the attitudes towards children in the first infant schools and her subsequent wish to change this. Brunszvik wanted to take care of and protect needy and innocent children. Brunszvik developed the theory of kindergartens as a result of influences from Pestalozzi (whose educational practice she had personally studied) and Rousseau whose educational axiom was the innocent child who needs to be cared for and protected while he is learning through experiences (see Chapter 2).

In 1837 a training institution for the further education of infant school teachers was established. After theoretical training, students could practise in a so-called *specimen asylum* (Kövér, 1987, p 19) similar to today's practice kindergartens. Those men (and only men), who had already obtained an education, were able to go through a year-long training period.

Building on the influence of European practices the first writings concerning Hungarian ECEC approaches can be attributed to István Wargha, the principal of the training school. The basis of his pedagogy is the 'children are taken as they are not as they should be' (Kövér, 1987, p 20) with the knowledge transmission being based on the interests of the child. Later Ferenc Ney would emphasise the importance of play as a form of education. He claimed: '*The infant school is not a school, therefore, its main task is not real teaching*' (Kövér, 1987, p 23). The focus on the interests of the child and play would remain a lasting legacy.

CASE STUDY

Amália Bezerédy

Among the first books for children is Amália Bezerédy's book: *Flóri's* (Kövér, 1987, p 27). The founder of infant schools wrote about morals and useful information in a poetic form for children. The book was a basic tool of emotional and moral education using a complex form of art (music, dance, literature, nursery rhymes, tales and fine art). Today's kindergarten practitioners have to study about this book during the history of kindergarten education. As a kindergarten teacher today there is an expectation that you will be undertaking some form or arts-based training (eg, music, singing). The arts are a core feature of the kindergarten teacher in Hungary.

In the 1860s and 1870s Friedrich Fröbel's pedagogical principles also became influential (see Chapters 2 and 8). Fröbel's philosophy aimed to develop children through childlike activities with the help of tools invented by him and according to his prescriptions. It was Fröbel's influence to call institutions dealing with children *kindergartens* – children's garden. From this point on the previously used infant school was changed to kindergarten. Teachers were called gardeners of children and mainly women were involved in working with children.

According to Kövér (1987, p 33), Fröbel's pedagogy along with Hungarian influences established the national kindergarten education. Fröbel's educational system was combined with national features and ideas, for instance, the use of many of Fröbel's tools were co-ordinated with the features of Hungarian kindergartens, but many pedagogues thought playfulness to be more important than the rigid prescriptions. This claim increased emphasis on Hungarian peculiarities as a result of the reform period of the early nineteenth century expressing an interest in the folk culture that features in the Hungarian national conscience. The appearance of folk games and folk poetry was supported by our national ethnic politics as well. While Hungarian folk values have fluctuated depending on the political period, they are a feature of Hungarian kindergarten education.

Critical questions

» *What are the national features that you feel are represented in ECEC in your home context?*

» *Do you think other countries would identify with these features in any way?*

CASE STUDY

The kindergarten pedagogue

When translated from Hungarian into English the name of the person working in the kindergarten is the 'kindergarten pedagogue' '*óvodapedagógus*' (used for both sexes). However, the philosophy, approach and understanding of the kindergarten pedagogue do not equate to be the same as the English nursery school or preschool teacher. It is not appropriate to refer to a nursery school teacher in the Hungarian context. That is why kindergarten pedagogues do not refer themselves as a 'teacher' '*tanár*' as they do not teach children directly (how to write and read) but they teach them through playing. '*Nevelés*' in Hungarian is a holistic concept, relating to pedagogy, but cannot directly translate. 'Education' in English is a close match, but it has a wider meaning, closer to upbringing (see Kaga, 2010).

After the Austro-Hungarian Compromise of 1867, economic and civilian changes resulted in recognition for institutional education. The number of kindergartens rose and there was a greater need for the unification in their activities. After the state regulation of public schools, regulation of kindergartens was made as well. In 1891 the Law of Infant Care appeared (Act XV of 1891). The role of the kindergarten was prescribed and those working in kindergartens fulfilled the role. Children aged three to six years old attended where there was availability. The Act made it clear that there was no place for scholastic education in kindergartens and there was an emphasis on folk traditions and the use of natural materials found in Hungary, as advocated by Sándor Peres. Compared to his predecessors working in kindergarten pedagogy, he mainly worked on the importance of games, illustration, kindergarten schedule and methodological advice. The law also ensured the development of training institutions.

Despite the focus on Hungarian Traditions, at the beginning of the twentieth century the study of children movement in Hungarian kindergarten pedagogy was influenced by foreigners (Hall, Baldwin, Stern, Terriere, Compayre). Among the theoreticians in the study of children movement we have to mention the father of the movement, László Nagy, and in the field of kindergarten pedagogy: Károly Ballai, László Nógrády, Leo Exner. The broader knowledge about children and psychology added to pedagogical knowledge and helped to get to know the personality of children better. On the basis of the new knowledge, games, activities and regard for the features of childhood were given greater emphasis. The representatives of the movement wanted to have the new knowledge domesticated faster and so they organised lectures and courses, published papers about theoretical and practical methods and conducted research.

Political and social changes after World War I

The end of World War I was a landmark for Hungary in many respects. The country became a small nation having been a European empire. Hungarian people felt a sense of loss and injustice as, due to the Trianon Treaty of 1920, Hungary lost two-thirds of its territory and inhabitants. Most of its industrial facilities, railways and mineral resources fell beyond the new boundaries of the country. Following this Treaty, Hungarian nursery history can be divided into two distinct periods:

1. 1920–34/36 – the period of relatively independent kindergartens; and

2. 1934/36–45 – the period of growing state influence.

The first period was not characteristic of the school system:

> It is not surprising that the child image elements of the new trends of reform pedagogy that put the primeval power of child soul, the spontaneity and productive fantasy of children on a pedestal easily fitted in the romantic traditions of the 19th century pre-school pedagogy.
>
> (Pukánszky, 2005, p 711)

In other words, the perception of nursery education kept its existing romantic features and, after the turn of the century, complemented them with new approaches to pedagogy, such as the work of Montessori. These two effects simultaneously prevailed for a long time (1920–36), including against the political and schooling efforts of the 1940s.

Sándor Imre and Elemér Kenyeres were two of the important educators of the period as the chairman and secretary of the professional organisation of kindergarten pedagogues (National Association of Kindergarten Pedagogues). This association supported the professional journal *Kisdednevelés*. The active presence of Sándor Imre in the world of nursery school pedagogy was a loose tie to the leading ideology of the period: cultural advantage through national education system. The foundation of this concept was laid down by Imre in the early years of the century, (1904 – Count István Széchenyi's Ideas of Education; 1912 – Education of the Nation), whereby the nation was considered a kind of educational unit, which well fitted the policy of *cultural advantage* represented by Kuno Klebersberg, Minister of Culture in the early 1920s. Cultural advantage symbolised the efforts to raise the Hungarian society above its neighbouring nations in moral and cultural senses following post-war losses.

The Montessori effect

Sándor Várnai published a description of Montessori pedagogy in the professional journal *Kisdednevelés* before World War I (Várnai 1912 cited in Kövér, 1987, p 66). However, the Italian idea and practice began to spread only in the late 1920s following Erzsébet Béláváry-Burchard taking part in an international Montessori course in 1923 and returning to Hungary to organise her own institution. She opened the first Hungarian Montessori nursery school in her parents' five-room house in 1927 (Sztrinkó, 2009, p 127). Erzsébet Burchard translated a substantial number of Montessori's documents into Hungarian therefore making them accessible for the wider public. The translations, along with the work of Pál Bardócz, greatly contributed to the spread of the Montessori pedagogy (Kövér, 1987, p 67). Bardócz was particularly influential in blending together important elements from the Montessori method and from the romantic tradition. '*He also drew the reader's attention to the fact that our pedagogic work can be successful only if we study the personality of the child in the greatest possible depth*' (Bardócz, 1928, p 18 cited by Pukánszky, 2005, p 709). Bardócz took over the Montessori principle saying that the development of the mental abilities can be reached only through the development of the senses. Bardócz also emphasised the role of music in education along with talks, poems, playing, physical exercise and drawing (Bardócz, 1928).

By the middle of the century the romantic child-centredness of reform pedagogy was gradually pushed into the background due to changing views on kindergarten pedagogy. Pukánszky says that as a result of the above tendencies:

> In the course of the century the main role of nursery schools gradually altered into preparation for school or in a wider sense, preparation for life.
>
> (Pukánszky, 2005, p 712)

In 1926 a significant change took place in the training of kindergarten pedagogues: the two-year training was lengthened to a four-year one. Good or excellent grades as well as appropriate musical and physical abilities were all requirements for admission to the training institutions. The fourth year meant the practical training of students. Due to all the above, a significant quality improvement took place in the Hungarian kindergarten pedagogue training between the two world wars (Sztrinkó, 2009, p 135).

Political influences in the 1930s

In 1936 the administration and control of nursery school teaching were transferred from the Minister of Religion and Public Education to the authority of the Minister of Public Administration. This resolution removed nursery schools from the public education system and transferred them to the borderline of social politics and public health as the operative control of nursery schools became the task of the chief health officer. Furthermore, in some villages nursery schools practically became childcare institutions as the primary function became providing social services for poor children instead of educating them. As a result of the above, the group size significantly grew in several places (even groups of 60–80 children) and the motivation for getting warm food on a daily basis overruled all other aims and functions.

The alternative to shifting towards the right: the folk tradition

Parallel with placing nursery schools under the authority of the Ministry of Public Administration, stronger and stronger national controls shaped the operation of institutions from the perspective of professional politics. From the 1930s, an alternative Hungarian trend appeared, placing folk traditions at the centre of education. The major representatives of this tendency were: Sándor Imre (previously introduced as a national educator), the internationally renowned composer and music scholar Zoltán Kodály, and Gyula Illyés who integrated folk tales into nursery school education. Kodály's 'Music in the nursery school' was a symbolic opening of the period in 1941 (Sztrinkó, 2009, p 138). After World War II, the Kodály method gained ground not only in nurseries but also in primary schools all over the world. However, the attempts made by the supporters of the folk-national trend could not lead to real success for another 50 years due to World War II and the one dimensional and autocratic Soviet influence that followed.

Two decades of Soviet-Russian kindergarten pedagogy in Hungary (1948–71)

After a short, temporary, relatively free period between 1947 and 1949, the one party Stalinist system was established in a swift manner that brought to Hungary the world of the Soviet-type terror in the form of deportations, show trials, ideological constraints and a penetrating personal cult. In 1953, Stalin died and the dictatorship became more moderate in Hungary. In 1956, a revolution broke out in Hungary that was taken down by the Soviet army. János Kádár became the first man of the country – he governed the country for more than 30 years (1956–88), in the course of which he focused on decreasing social tensions and setting up a more peaceful version of communism often called 'goulash communism' (goulash is a name of a traditional Hungarian soup).

In 1948 schools and kindergartens were nationalised. In the following decades the number of kindergartens rapidly increased due to an increased birth rate and women's mass employment being required by the forced Stalinist industrialism: 'the socialist work ethic'. Kindergartens became recognised for their role in educating the 'socialist citizens' of the future (and their families). From 1949 the Soviet pattern and the setting of it as a requirement came into prominence. The published literature was *'infested by the spirit of the Soviet ideology and the Soviet pedagogy itself'*. *'Education became a "slave" to the politics of the party'* (Pukánszky and Németh, 1996, p 658). The productive, disciplined and obedient man was at the centre of education ideals (Golnhofer, 2004, p 125). This meant that the previous Hungarian education approach and its nationalistic folk feature disappeared and was modified according to the Marxist quire.

In 1950, Bleher's *Organized Sessions in Kindergarten* was translated and given to the kindergartners, defining the approach of the Hungarian kindergartens for years. This book had been written for Soviet kindergartners and it was not even questioned whether it was applicable within the Hungarian context. The Hungarian introduction of the book (no one knows the author) phrased the spirit of the Hungarian kindergartens in a long-term view. *'The kindergarten is not only setting the basis of the many-sided socialist man but it also gives a methodical preparation for school education'* (Bleher, 1950, p 3). Kindergartens with a public education role were fundamentally considered as a preparatory for school.

Critical questions

The introduction of one curriculum for all Soviet countries raises questions as to whether it is possible or appropriate to try and adopt one system across several countries.

» *While the Soviet period is an extreme example of curricula spanning borders, do you think countries can adopt the same curriculum?*

» *What do you think might influence the potential for curriculums spanning borders?*

In 1953 a law reorganised kindergartens, assigning them to schools due to their role in preparing for school education. *'The significance of the 1953 law is indeed that the institution of the kindergarten had become [an] integral part of our education system'* (Kövér, 2004, p 68). The *Methodological Letters* (which was actually opposite to the plural as there was only one issue published in this series) was published in 1953. It tried to strengthen the establishment of a uniform approach of kindergartens with the above-mentioned legal background. The *Methodological Letters* were about compulsory sessions which were the primary tools for education and teaching children. The letters were actually the kindergarten adaptations of the school timetables. The interests of the children were only considered when it was the task of the kindergartner to capture the children's attention. Even in free-time children could choose something to do but *'it could not be done without the directing role of the kindergartner'* (Methodological Letters – Kindergarten Sessions, 1953, p 4). Besides ordinary topics kindergartners had to consider the requirements of the actual politics. The smallest children had to recognise Lenin, Stalin and Rákosi from pictures but the older children had to tell who they were ('they are our leaders who love children a lot'). Co-operation with families did not even occur within the responsibilities of the Ministry of Education.

In 1957 *Education in the Kindergarten* was published, containing the experiences of the past 10 years of socialist pedagogical practices. Kindergartens were recognised as the lowest level of the public education system. A new and extensive element in the document was that it required kindergartners to take the age specialties and needs of 3–6 year olds into consideration when 'thoroughly instructing', so that the tools and methods would ensure the versatile development of children. The focus on the needs of a specific age group proved to be a reform idea. Psychology had been considered a remnant of the 1950s civil society (there was no psychology training), but after the revolution of 1956 Ferenc Mérei, the most widely known representative of children's psychology, was rehabilitated from his silenced state and training of psychology started in universities in the 1960s.

In the guideline the 'special significance of playing' was recognised though only for the sake of strengthening the role of education.

> *In a kindergarten where kids can play there is a calmer and more disciplined atmosphere, and children pay more attention during the compulsory sessions.*
>
> (Education in the Kindergarten, a Guideline
> for Kindergartners, 1957, p 58)

However, in the case of planning the sessions it was taking on the previous mechanisms introduced back in 1953.

Education in the Kindergarten from 1957 was characterised by the adaptation of the characteristic of school learning. The preparatory role of kindergartens was an unquestionable approach for many decades. This approach, however, also helped strengthen the prestige of kindergarten pedagogy and kindergartner career, leading to 1959, when kindergartner training featured in higher education programmes – though the college level was only reached two decades later.

The ideology is changed to professionalism (1971–89)

After 1957 more work was done in kindergarten pedagogy and psychology that raised attention to the characteristics and education of kindergarten children. After collecting and evaluating previous kindergarten practices there was support that they should be changed. Psychology had again become a recognised science in Hungary and even with much selection there were more books available in Hungary from more and more Western authors. Along with the Soviet-Russian work of Elkonyin and Vygotszky, works of Piaget and Wallon had also become very popular.

The *Education in the Kindergarten* (1957) national kindergarten document was replaced after 15 years with a new programme that was different in its ideology and content (Vág, 1979, p 160). The goal setting of this document regulating Hungarian kindergarten pedagogy shows a deliberate change:

> *The goal of kindergarten education is part of the uniform socialist education system. It aims to help the diverse and harmonious development of 3–6 year old children.*
>
> (Kindergarten Education Programme, 1971, p 9)

In spite of the compulsory adjective 'socialist' the document emphasises children's personal development.

Contrary to the previous documents the programme mentions family rights and composed the common responsibility. The concept accepts that the same child is educated by the family and the kindergarten but *'for the sake of the uniformity of influences it is the kindergarten that is the initiative'* (Kindergarten Education Programme, 1971, p 11).

'Playing is the primary activity of children at kindergarten age' (Kindergarten Education Programme, 1971, p 77). The Programme gave rise to claims that it can be regarded as the first serious professional step towards a child-centred approach. It is important to mention that the new document advocated recognising the individual experiences coming from the children's families and common experiences from outside the kindergarten (the doctor's, shop, market), while also increasing the freedom and ability to choose playing activities for children. The children and their primary activities (play) were at the centre, but not equal to the main political ideology.

One of the results of the recognition of age characteristics in kindergarten is that they introduced a new way of learning – the system of informal sessions along with compulsory ones. While the education system preserved the hegemonic, all defining roles, neither the content nor the development level to be reached by children had to be taken so stiffly that the requirements would be fulfilled in all children. The approach and opportunity of individual management was present within the programme.

We cannot forget that in spite of the above-mentioned positive changes, the compulsory frameworks of education kept many of the previous didactical elements. Nonetheless, the programme of 1971 can be regarded as a milestone because it opened the way for professional thinking that recognised aspects of children and incorporated them into the pedagogical logic.

CASE STUDY

Higher education training at the University of Debrecen

The wide range of kindergarten systems and the appreciation that those working with children need to have a more intensive scientific and psycho-social judgement is recognised by a demand for having kindergartner training at college level. In 1983, in Hajdúböszörmény, there was a model started with a 2+1 year: a two-year-long training programme with an extra year of learning while working, in recognition of the skill set needed by those working with young children. In 1985, the law was born which made the higher education studies of the kindergartners to be a three-year college-level programme. At present (2014), according to the Bologna process, kindergartners take part in a three-year-long BA programme in Hungary. The training college in Hajdúböszörmény still exists as part of the University of Deberecen, teaching future kindergarteners about child-centred, play-based approaches, characterised by Hungarian folk culture.

From the change of regime to the present (1984–2014)

In 1985 Mihail Gorbacsov became the first man of the Soviet Union and started to reform the Soviet system radically. The reforms led to the disintegration of the Soviet Union and the communist block. Hungary became one of the lead fighters of the changes. In the summer of 1989, we were the first to remove the so-called Iron Curtain, that enabled free travelling to Western countries and on 23 October 1989, on the memorial day of the 1956 Revolution, the third Republic of Hungary was proclaimed. By this act, Hungary had stepped into the row of democratic countries. It was not just a physical but intellectual removal of the Iron Curtain: from the beginning of the 1990s there were more connections made with the professional audience of the previously forbidden countries and Western works of pedagogy and psychology became available as well.

The political, social and intellectual changes did not leave kindergartens untouched either. A new kindergarten programme was established in 1989, as a result of the improved version of the previous one. The Improved Kindergarten Program (IKP) still meant a uniform, compulsory programme for all kindergartens to help with the diverse and harmonious development of 3–6/7-year-old children. It is obvious that the age was extended, as *flexible schooling* had been legalised which meant starting school according to maturity not age. Therefore, kindergartens took up the educating of those children who did not meet the rigid criteria of school maturity by the age of six or those whose parents asked to have one more year in kindergarten education for their children.

In the new programme the psychological influence continued. Compared to the previous wordings it was a new element to set the requirement from the kindergarten to ensure 'an emotional shell' for the development of a child. Kindergartens focused on children's emotional security and assured children of their dignity and legal rights. Children's rights were a new feature, so there was little detail surrounding them. Pedagogical ethics was also mentioned, which implied handling information obtained from parents.

Playing, working and learning

The programme defined three main activities: playing, working, learning. Playing was the absolute priority: '*Playing is the primary and most basic activity that infiltrates all the other activities of the child*' (Kindergarten Education Programme, 1989, p 9). Learning was regarded as a broad activity, influenced by psychology and understandings of child development. As such there is an understanding of formal learning, as seen in previous decades, but also recognition of the value of learning from spontaneous situations. The programme recognised earlier saw ideas of the role of the kindergarten in preparing children for school, but it defended against the school doctrines within the kindergarten environment by offering a proactive solution:

> *The staff of the kindergarten should make it their task, if needed, to have an impact on the receptive school with their children centred approach and methods.*
>
> (Kindergarten Education Programme, 1989, p 279)

Expecting the kindergarten pedagogue to have an impact on school proved to be a utopian Ideal; it had laid down the foundations of a child-centred, democratic educational institution which was built on the unprompted activities of the children.

In the 1990s, the fall of the Iron Curtain resulted in a new legal foundation for Hungary as a result of the new social and political system. As a result a new law was needed for the whole public education system. The Hungarian Parliament accepted the LXXIX Act on public education in 1993. The law legitimated the work of public education institutions with more maintenance (whether state, private, or church founded), eliminated the ideological one-sidedness from state institutions, forbade political activities and enabled pluralism in pedagogy. It states that kindergarten is part of *the professionally independent public education institutions* (Act LXXIX of 1993 on Public Education). Kindergarten education remains part of the free public education system. The kindergarten accepts children from the age of three, but having accepted the European practice of compulsory education, it is compulsory to take part in the kindergarten education from the age of five for all children. Another important paragraph in the Act that affected the professional work of all kindergartens was that (similarly to the school curricula) there is no demand for kindergartens to have a concise programme describing the whole system and its contents, as had been seen historically. Kindergarteners can make a pedagogical programme based on the National Kindergarten Education Program or can choose from recommended pedagogical programmes (Act LXXIX of 1993 on Public Education 45, p 1). This meant a fundamental change for all the kindergartens as their programme writing had no antecedent in the recent history of Hungarian kindergartens and composing their own local educational programme required serious responsibility and professional struggle from all kindergarten pedagogues.

The National Core Program of Kindergarten Education (Core Program for short) was developed in 1996. It is a short framework-like document determining common principles and aspects of Hungarian kindergartens. This new central programme was a clear break from the regulation of the documents of the state socialist era in its approach as well as its form. One of its important features is that it does not have any curricular requirement, so the kindergartens could assemble the contents of their local educational activities in relation to what they thought to be important for their local educational context. The approach ensured the characteristics of children were purposefully put into prominence, being strongly child- (and play-) centred.

After the annunciation of the Act, kindergartens got three years to work out and authorise their local educational programmes that respect the principles of the Core Program and introduce it to the everyday practice of the kindergartens. The Core Program liberated kindergarteners in a way not seen before. The Core Program, thanks to its child-centred and framework-like nature, let the propagation of different concepts of reform and alternative pedagogy: Freinet, Waldorf, Montessori pedagogy are present mainly, and an American programme called Step by Step. Besides these, many kindergartens have made their modern and respective programmes or applied and adopted existing kindergarten programmes. The process of application is helped by groups called Qualified (professionally monitored, filtered) Program Groups that are freely available to kindergartens.

In 2011 there was a new law that made the administration of Hungarian schools centralised again (Act CXC of 2011 on Public Education). Kindergartens are still free to develop their approaches that fit the local educational context. A new element in the law made attendance at kindergarten compulsory from the age of three in order to ensure access to early childhood education and care as of 1 September 2014. The law provides a possibility for delaying entry until the child turns five in cases where the parent applies for an exemption. The aim is to help to reduce the negative associations of socio-cultural and social-economic disadvantages by offering kindergarten care to support children's cognitive development.

Critical questions

»   *European frameworks have encouraged the introduction of compulsory early education, such as that in Hungary. Do you think that children should have to go to kindergarten (preschool)?*

»   *Do you see the role of preschool as being about reducing the negative associations of socio-cultural disadvantage, supporting cognitive development or both?*

»   *Do you think there are other roles for early education?*

Critical reflections

Those children now entering kindergarten at the age of three (and continuing until six or seven) will encounter a system that is child-centred and professionally colourful. The influences on the Hungarian approach are shaped by both its political history and its location within Europe and the Europeans who shared their thinking on children, childhood, child development and education (in its broadest sense). In many ways this does not set Hungary aside from any other European country, but what we regard as unique to Hungary is its ability to look to theories and philosophies from across the world and to combine these with a strong focus on (and love of) our traditions. The folk traditions that we first discussed being of influence in the 1800s and that we have seen overshadowed at times in our socio-political history are now an important part of our kindergarten education. This is most prominently reflected in the requirement for those undertaking training to become a kindergarten pedagogue to also have skills in music and/or singing. The result is a pedagogical approach with its own melodic soundtrack.

Further reading

Korintus, M (2008) Early Childhood Education and Care in Hungary: Challenges and Recent Developments. *International Journal of Child Care and Education Policy*, 2(2): 43–52.

This paper offers a useful overview of the more political developments of ECEC in Hungary, but also supports what we have discussed in this chapter in terms of philosophy and what influences current ECEC provision in Hungary.

Ovácsné Bakosi, E (2013) Hungary: Kindergarten as a Public Education Institution, in Georgeson, J and Payler, J (eds) *International Perspectives On Early Childhood Education And Care*. Maindenhead: McGraw Hill.

This chapter talks more about the curriculum in Hungarian kindergartens, but it discusses the core principles of our curriculum reflecting the themes that we have raised in this chapter in terms of the philosophical ideas that underpin the Hungarian approach.

References

Bardócz, P (1928) *A magyar kisdednevelés vezérkönyve*. Budapest: Székesfőváros Házinyomdája.

Bleher, F N (1950) *Szervezett foglalkozások az óvodában*. Budapest: Közoktatási Kiadó.

Golnhofer, E (2004) *Hazai pedagógiai nézetek 1945–1949*. Pécs: Iskolakultúra.

Kaga, Y, Bennett, J and Moss, P (2010) *Caring and Learning Together*. Paris: Unesco. [online] Also available at: http://unesdoc.unesco.org/images/0018/001878/187818e.pdf (accessed 28 Aug 2014).

Kindergarten Education Programme (1971) *Az Óvodai Nevelés Programja*. Tankönyvkiadó: Budapest.

Kindergarten Education Programme (1989) *Az Óvodai Nevelés Programja*. Országos Pedagógiai Intézet.

Kövér, S (1987) *Az értelmi nevelés története óvodáinkban 1828–1975 között*. Budapest: Közgazdasági és Jogi Könyvkiadó.

Kövér, S (2004) Kell-e mennünk Európába? – A magyar és az európai óvodai rendszer kapcsolata és sajátos vonásai 1828–1998 között. *Neveléstörténet*, 3–4: 63–7.

Methodological Letters – Kindergarten Sessions (1953) The 'Education in the Kindergarten' national kindergarten document (1957).

Módszertani Levelek – Óvodai foglalkozások (1953) *Az Oktatásügyi Miniszter rendeletére*. Tankönyvkiadó: Budapest.

National Core Programme of Kindergarten Education (1996) *Óvodai Nevelés Országos Alapprogramja*. SEMIC Interprint.

Nevelőmunka az óvodában, Útmutatás óvónők számára (1957). Tankönyvkiadó: Budapest, p 258.

Pukánszky, B (2005) A gyermekről alkotott kép változásai az óvoda történetében. *Educatio*, 4: 700–11.

Pukánszky, B and Németh, A (1996) *Neveléstörténet*. Budapest: Nemzeti Tankönyvkiadó

Sztrinkó, N (2009) *Óvó-iskola, gyermekkert, óvoda: a kisgyermekkor neveléstörténete*. Debrecen: Didakt.

Vág, O (1979) *Óvoda és óvodapedagógia*. Tankönyvkiadó: Budapest.

10 ECEC in the Philippines: a multicultural and multilingual context

GREG TABIOS PAWILEN

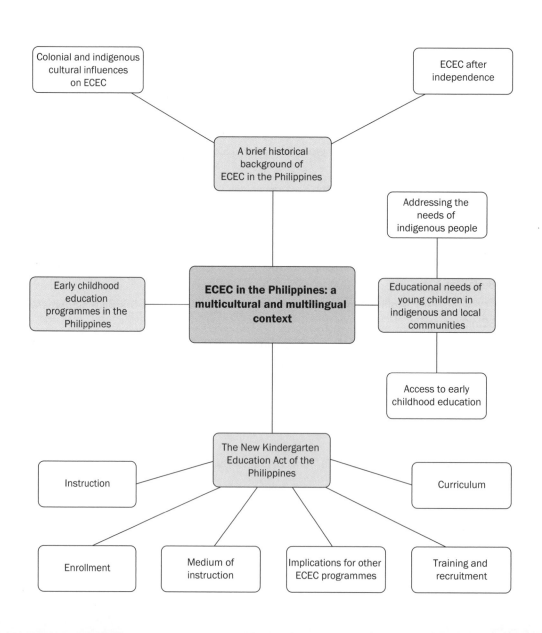

Introduction

This chapter shares experiences and challenges of early childhood education and care (ECEC) in the Philippines. The country is an archipelago of more than 7100 islands, inhabited by millions of Filipinos from more than 77 major ethno-linguistic groups (Peralta, 2003). Filipino children belong to different cultural groups, including indigenous communities. The country, through collaborative effort and commitment from the government and private sectors, aims to provide education that is culturally relevant and responsive to all Filipino children.

The constitution of the Republic of the Philippines recognises the right of every Filipino child to access quality education and training (Republic of the Philippines Constitution, 1987). The Philippines also shares the global commitments of the 2000 Dakar Framework for Action (UNESCO, 2000), which includes expanding and improving comprehensive ECEC especially for the most vulnerable and disadvantaged children, as elaborated in Education For All (EFA) monitoring report (UNESCO, 2007).

A brief historical background of ECEC in the Philippines

Colonial and indigenous cultural influences on ECEC

The tradition of educating and caring for young children in the Philippines is surely older than the founding of the country itself. The early inhabitants of the country developed a unique system characterised by their cultural beliefs, values and experiences; in the home parents (both mother and father) did their best to collaboratively raise and nurture their children based on family and social values. Parents served as the first teachers and caregivers for their children. The curriculum was cultural experience that placed strong emphasis on family and social values, history, spirituality and various life skills needed for everyday life.

Muslims in the Philippines established schools or *madrasah* in the fourteenth century when children aged five to seven began to study the Qur'an under an elder who was either an Alim (Islam scholar) or an Uztadz (male teacher of Islamic Values and Arabic language). The pupils visited the teacher's house or the *madrasah* and were taught for free. The lessons consisted of reciting the Qur'an and learning Arabic language and Islamic values.

When the Spaniards colonised the country in the sixteenth century, the Roman Catholic Church through its missionaries and priests organised learning sessions for young children to learn Catholic prayers and religious practices (Magpuri, 2002). The priests served as teachers for young children, who were expected to memorise simple Spanish terms and Latin prayers that they never truly understood. This was the practice throughout 333 years of Spanish colonisation of the Philippines. Although private Catholic schools were established in the country, there are no accounts of preschools or childcare programmes established for Filipinos; the Spanish government never took this seriously.

Missionary schools

After the Treaty of Paris in 1898, the Spanish government surrendered the Philippine Islands to the United States. The new colonial masters had a vision of establishing a public school system across the whole country to prepare Filipinos for democracy and self-governance. They brought with them missionaries from different Protestant churches who started various pioneering missionary works in different parts of the archipelago. American Protestant churches established many schools in different provinces to teach young children basic (English) language and literacy and Bible study. Missionaries acted as both teachers and mentors to Filipinos serving as teaching assistants.

In 1923, Harris Memorial College, a school established by the Methodist Church, pioneered the first formal kindergarten in the Philippines (National Historical Institute, 1993). Since the Philippines was then still under US government control, the curriculum was patterned on existing US early childhood curricula (Harris Memorial College, 2007). The curriculum, with English as the medium of instruction, focused on early literacy, arithmetic, music and movement, and religious instruction. Instructional materials such as books and songs were brought from the US. Local Protestant churches started to operate kindergartens as a part of their ministry for younger children across the country.

Jungle schools

World War II temporarily paralysed several ECEC programmes and many schools were either destroyed or turned into military camps by the Japanese. However, individual accounts tell of Filipinos establishing *jungle schools* for young children, in a collective effort to divert children's attention from the fears, stresses and pains of war. Jungle schools were conducted in the mountains in hiding from Japanese soldiers. Volunteers taught the alphabet and simple mathematics, told young children stories and provided food for them to share.

ECEC after independence

After the war, the Philippines finally gained its independence in 1946, and the mission of early childhood education continued. However, there was a problem – lack of teachers and facilities. Harris remained the only school in the country offering teacher education for kindergarten for some decades. The country was just starting to rebuild from the ruins of war. The establishment of primary schools and institutions for orphans was the priority; private schools and church-led schools were the few institutions to continue provision for ECEC.

For many decades, early childhood education remained optional, operated almost entirely by private schools. Most young children in early childhood education came from middle- and upper-class families; the government concentrated on supporting childcare programmes and developing educational policies for elementary to tertiary level.

In 1991, the *Barangay* (Village) Level Total Protection of Children Act became law, requiring all local government units to establish a daycare centre in every village. This law was instrumental in helping poorer parents provide for their children's educational and health needs. Daycare programmes also included basic literacy to support young children not enrolled in a kindergarten. A social worker or a professional from the community was assigned to serve as teacher and programme co-ordinator for daycare centres.

The beginning of the twenty-first century brought substantial reforms and developments in early childhood education in the Philippines. The Department of Education (DepEd) National EFA Committee identified early childcare programmes as critical to achieving EFA goals by 2015. The Early Child Care and Development (ECCD) Act of 2000 created the ECCD Council to undertake comprehensive and sustainable multi-sectoral and inter-agency collaboration for early childhood care, development and education of young Filipino children. It recognised the importance and particular needs of early childhood, affirmed parents as primary caregivers and the child's first teachers and established parenting programmes and projects.

The most recent reform in 2012 formally recognised kindergarten education as part of the education system of the Philippines. This is described in more detail later, but has completely changed the landscape of early childhood education and care across the whole country. Currently, kindergartens in the Philippines are growing like mushrooms. These schools are either operated by the government or owned by private organisations and individuals; ECEC has become a business. Public and private kindergartens across the country are now under the supervision of the Department of Education, while daycare centres are under the Department of Social Welfare and Development. This offers a systematic way of providing quality services for ECEC in the Philippines, regulating important policies and ensuring quality welfare programmes for Filipino children.

Early childhood education programmes in the Philippines

With the growth of preschool education in the Philippines, different educational philosophies have been introduced based on progressive educational theories and models developed and implemented in Western countries (Lupdag, 1999). The influence of computer technology, particularly in urban areas, and the growing prominence of Gardner's Theory of Multiple Intelligence have also influenced how preschool curricula are organised and taught. In general, learner-centred philosophies dominate educational theory for early childhood in the Philippines. However, different early childhood education programmes are offered by different schools and educational institutions in various parts of the country.

- *Church-related Preschool Programmes*: several religious groups, mostly Christian churches, established their own preschool institutions throughout the country. Their primary goal is to provide an education integrating teaching Christian values and religious practices.

- *Kindergarten Madrasah Programme* is offered to Muslim children enrolled in public Arabic Language and Islamic Values Education (ALIVE) programmes or private schools implementing the standard Madrasah curriculum.

- *Montessori Approach*: is widely accepted across the country. The Montessori curriculum focuses on daily living, sensorial activities and materials, and conceptual activities and materials (didactic and self-correcting). Children work individually or in small groups (see Chapter 4). Teacher preparation or training is needed.

- *Waldorf Programme*: the philosophy emphasises the development of the whole child and the goal is to encourage children to become self-motivated. Play and interaction with others are emphasised, as well as multi-sensory experiences and creative art. Teachers are mother figures who work to understand individual temperaments.

- *Progressive Preschools*: the child is viewed as a scientist – always curious to explore, learn, observe and develop new ideas. Attention is given to development of competence, individuality, socialisation and integration. Play is the means to construct and reconstruct knowledge and the school is a community of learners.

- *The University of the Philippines Child Development Center Integrated Core Curriculum Model* is the laboratory school of the College of Home Economics for preschool education. This model advocates a holistic view of the child within a developmental perspective, with teacher as learning facilitator. The curriculum puts emphasis on the inter-relatedness between all areas of learning and learning through play.

- *Traditional Preschool Programme*: these schools follow a curriculum with heavy emphasis on learning several academic subjects, with the aim of preparing learners for Grade I. Children use textbooks and activity books in the classroom, pencil and paper tests are administered and numerical grades given to each child at the end of term. Most private schools follow this programme, due to parents' demands.

- *DepEd Preschool Programmes*: the Department of Education (DepEd) provides a standard for preschool education with several learning areas including: communication skills, numeracy skills, sensory-perceptual skills, socio-emotional development, and motor and creative development – very similar to the traditional approach.

- *Daycare Programmes*: the Department of Social Welfare and Development (DSWD), in co-operation with local government units, operates daycare programmes for children in local communities. Although focused on childcare, basic skills like socialising, communicating, writing, reading and simple mathematics are also included to help parents who cannot send their children to a regular private preschool.

- *Indigenous Peoples' Education* aims to promote the preservation, recognition, promotion and protection of the rights of indigenous people and their cultural identity and heritage. This type of education incorporates histories, languages, indigenous knowledge systems and practices as well as indigenous peoples' social, economic and cultural priorities and aspirations (DepEd Order No. 32, s 2012).

- *Headstart Programme for the Gifted*: a comprehensive programme in public schools that focuses on addressing the needs and nurture of gifted children.

- *Early Intervention Programme for Children with Disabilities* focuses on addressing the needs of young children with special needs. The programme provides services that will help special children to cope with everyday life.

- *Basic Literacy Programmes* include non-formal projects to help young children learn basic literacies especially reading, writing and mathematical skills. Both government and non-government organisations implement Basic Literacy Programmes, sometimes in collaboration. Some Basic Literacy Programmes and projects also include childcare components like health and nutrition programmes, values formation and child protection activities.

Critical questions

» *Why do you think there are so many different preschool programmes in the Philippines?*

» *Think about a topic like water; how might teachers working within the different programmes teach this differently?*

» *How might Gardner's Theory of Multiple Intelligence influence a preschool programme?*

Implementation of these early childhood education programmes needs qualified, committed teachers and childcare professionals and reviews of existing pre-service teacher education to respond to these different demands.

Educational needs of young children in indigenous and local communities

Addressing diversity is a major challenge for early childhood education teachers in the Philippines. Societies are becoming pluralistic with respect to race, ethnicity, religion, language, gender, sexual orientation and social class. Settings must be prepared to address diversity and associated issues. Diversity not only demands a new curriculum and instruction for learners, it also requires major reforms of pre-service teacher education and continuing professional development for existing kindergarten teachers to update their knowledge.

Addressing the needs of indigenous people

Many Filipino young children belong to different ethno-linguistic groups. The government recognises the right of every Filipino to access quality education regardless of race, ethnic background or culture (The Republic of the Philippines Constitution, 1987). *The Indigenous Peoples Rights Act* 1997 also recognises the right of indigenous people to an *integrated education system* that is relevant to their needs. This Act empowers indigenous local communities to preserve their culture, indigenous knowledge, traditions and customs, known as *community intellectual rights*, and provides a legal foundation for indigenous education and community-based curricula in the country.

CASE STUDY

Jean Ulay-Gudayan, kindergarten teacher to the Isnag tribe

I finished my degree in kindergarten education at Harris Memorial College in 1976. There I was taught that teaching is a calling; sharing our lives, talent and time in teaching young children is a ministry from God. After I graduated from college, I was assigned to teach kindergarten in different local and indigenous communities in the Philippines.

I was assigned to a community of Isnag Tribe in the Cordillera Mountains of Luzon. There were many young children who were eager to learn but there was no school. I talked to the community leaders and church people and presented my plan to set up a school. The people were so excited but they didn't have money to construct a building or buy instructional materials. I told them that money should not be a hindrance to a kindergarten school for young children.

We started learning under the shade of big trees while waiting for the community folks to finish constructing our classroom from bamboo and cogon grass. The curriculum focused on reading, writing, mathematics, science, nutrition and values. True enough, there were no instructional materials, so I tried my best to improvise, be creative and resourceful. I used tiny stones, bamboo sticks and leaves to teach counting. Mother Nature always provided us with natural objects, plants and animals to study science.

I also told Bible stories and local stories to young children to help them learn values. I taught them new and traditional folk songs for music. We learnt traditional dance and games and I also taught them how to sing simple church hymns. For our language class, I taught them how to read and write. I used their local language as medium of instruction.

There were no school uniforms. The young children came to school in their usual daily dress. I had to teach young children the value of cleanliness and personal hygiene. I also taught them about basic nutrition. The community could not afford to give me high salary. Young children and their parents always brought fruits, vegetable and other produce from Mother Nature as their love-gifts to me.

The greatest challenge for all of us came in the late 1980s. The village was caught up in insurgency war between rebels and government forces. Our classroom was destroyed and so we held classes under the trees and sometimes in a cave. Teaching and learning during those times was never easy. But I always remember my lesson from Harris that young children are precious gifts from God; they need to be nurtured and loved. For security reasons, I was asked to move to a different place but I simply couldn't leave the village, especially the young children – their voices during recitation, their songs, chants and prayers. I always heard them saying 'Ma'am Jean, dida kami panpanawan' (Ma'am Jean, please don't leave us).

Looking back, I realise that teaching young children in indigenous communities is a challenging and noble task. Apart from teaching, we perform many tasks as surrogate parents, principal, counsellor, school nurse and nanny for young children. We also serve as school registrar and, of course, everyday we serve as janitor to clean our classroom. It takes strong commitment and dedication to do all these tasks. We do our job without complaining about the low salary that we receive compared to our counterparts in the cities and other progressive communities. I sincerely believe that God is sending me in various places to teach and touch the lives of young children. Teaching kindergarten in indigenous communities is my mission.

A particular need of preschool education in the Philippines is a culturally relevant preschool curriculum (Pawilen and Sumida, 2007). Most preschool curricula used in many private schools are either directly adapted from abroad or influenced by foreign educational models. This means that young children learn concepts and topics that are not related to their local contexts and culture. Although mother-tongue-based multilingual education is currently implemented by the Department of Education, in many private schools English remains the language of instruction. Consequently, these practices contribute to the miseducation of Filipinos. Instructional materials should reflect the needs and culture of young children from local communities, particularly indigenous knowledge of the community; education institutions also need to develop and train teachers to work with such materials.

Critical questions

»   *Can you anticipate any challenges to the concept of community intellectual rights?*

»   *How transferrable do you think this kind of cultural capital is?*

»   *Which aspects of Jean's training did she draw on to help meet the needs of the children she was teaching?*

»   *Can you distinguish between vocation and mission?*

»   *How would you define miseducation? Can you think of an example from your own experience?*

Access to early childhood education

In a study I conducted in 2006, I found only 60 per cent of young children in each community attended preschool classes, in either daycare centres or private schools. There were several reasons why children did not attend preschool classes.

•   Parents couldn't afford to pay for their tuition fees.

•   Children were not motivated to go to school.

•   The school was too far from children's homes.

•   Parents viewed preschool education as unnecessary for young children.

The children who attended preschool classes in community schools belonged to poor or middle-class families; families who could afford to pay tuition fees sent their children to big schools in the town or city. Most children attending preschool classes in community schools went to school on foot (with accompanying parent) or by tricycle that served as transportation in lieu of school bus (Pawilen, 2006).

The new Kindergarten Education Act of the Philippines

The situation however changed drastically with implementation of The Kindergarten Act in 2012. Kindergarten was institutionalised as part of the Philippines basic education programme. Parents are now obliged by the state to send their children to kindergarten before elementary education and the state provides free tuition fees for public kindergarten. This has created a gigantic increase of enrollment in public kindergarten. Bringing kindergarten education to the grassroots offers the perfect opportunity to develop literacy levels, especially for young children from indigenous communities. This is in consonance with the EFA goals set by UNESCO (2000) to expand and improve early childhood care and education, especially for the most vulnerable and disadvantaged children by 2015.

The new law recognises kindergarten education as vital to Filipino children's academic and technical development but implementation has brought many challenges to educators and schools across the archipelago.

Curriculum

A new kindergarten curriculum in the Philippines that was released in December 2013 prescribes curriculum standards for the holistic development of Filipino children according to individual needs and socio-cultural background. The curriculum focuses on seven important domains:

1. values education;
2. physical health and motor development;
3. socio-emotional development;
4. social development;
5. language, literacy and communication;
6. mathematics; and
7. understanding the physical and natural environment.

Under the seven learning domains are curriculum standards and competencies that define what young children are expected to learn and develop as a result of learning. Topics under these seven domains are organised around five curricular themes:

1. myself;
2. my family;
3. my community;
4. my school; and
5. more things around me.

The new curriculum also provides opportunities for indigenous people and children with special needs to have a curriculum that is responsive to their needs.

Critical questions

» *How would you organise a topic to promote learning in each of the seven domains while incorporating one or more of the themes? Give an example and explain your thinking.*

» *Are there any other aspects of learning you would want to include?*

Instruction

In spite of the country's new curriculum standards, implementation of the new curriculum is still dominated by imported instructional and curriculum materials. Teaching strategies and lesson exemplars used in teaching young children are based on foreign pedagogical principles and theories. While it is important that young children should develop global competencies, there is a need to develop pedagogical models and principles that reflect the culture and context of Filipino children. Teachers and childcare workers also need proper training and assistance on how to implement the new curriculum to meet the needs, learning styles and culture of the young children they serve.

Medium of instruction

The law stipulates that early childhood education will be delivered in languages understood by the learners, as language plays a strategic role in shaping their formative years. For kindergarten and the first three years of elementary education, instruction, teaching materials and assessment shall be in the regional or native language of the learners, including Filipino sign language used by individuals with pertinent disabilities (Republic Act 10157). Teachers should therefore have the skills and competence to develop local or indigenous instructional materials and receive training in teaching in multicultural and multilanguage contexts. Preschool teachers and professionals working in childcare need high levels of cultural literacy to help them better respond to the needs and nature of all Filipino children.

Enrollment

Table 10.1 shows that, since 2008, enrollment in kindergarten continues to rise, especially in public schools.

For school year 2013–14, the Department of Education reported a total enrollment of 1,865,807 in about 38,631 public schools in the country. Though there is no available data for private schools for this school year, they also expect enrollment to increase. The main reason for the increase of enrollment in public schools is probably the free public education policy implemented by the Philippine government, and this trend is likely to continue.

The steady increase of enrollment in kindergarten leads to different challenges: the need for more classrooms, instructional materials and other facilities; hiring new teachers in public

Table 10.1 Enrollment data for kindergarten in the Philippines from 2008 to 2013

Type of schools	2008–09	2009–10	2010–11	2011–12	2012–13
Public	746,448	1,054,200	1,224,173	1,683,293	1,773,505
Private	428,653	420,444	426,059	428,064	428,981
Total	1,175,101	1,474,644	1,650,232	2,111,357	2,202,486

Source: Basic Education Statistics (Department of Education, 2013).

and private schools; access – the establishment of kindergarten in local and indigenous communities.

Training and recruitment

The new curriculum has created a growing demand for qualified kindergarten teachers to teach in public and private schools across the country. The majority of the teachers are female and more male involvement in early childhood education is needed. The law specifies that kindergarten teachers should pass the Licensure Exam for Teachers in the Philippines. As of this school year 2014–15, there are about 228,502 public elementary schools in the Philippines. All these schools have kindergarten education programmes. During the first year of implementation in 2013, selected elementary teachers were trained to manage preschool classes and paid with modest honoraria. Elsewhere, local government hired temporary preschool teachers to teach in public schools.

Qualified early childhood education teachers are also needed to teach in multicultural and multilingual settings, including indigenous communities. The government policy on mother-tongue-based multilingual education poses challenges; it requires that teachers should at least be native of a particular place in order to speak the language and use the mother tongue as a medium of instruction in classes. There is therefore a need to train teachers from different indigenous groups.

Developing high-quality teachers who understand the nature and needs of young children in local communities is important for local communities. Teachers play a crucial role in designing and implementing curricula for young children. They also serve as second parents to young learners, especially in preschool. Most of the preschool teachers in local communities are not trained, or prepared for the various challenges of teaching children in local communities (Pawilen, 2011). These challenges call for the development of teaching and professional competencies to respond to the needs of different learners for teachers and other professionals involved in early childhood education and childcare across the country.

Private kindergarten teachers in public schools received higher salaries than in most private schools because of the Salary Standardization Law for government employees. A newly-hired public school teacher receives monthly pay of 18,549.00 pesos while an ordinary private school teacher in a small private school receives a monthly salary of 5000.00 (£1=73 pesos). The big difference between salaries and benefits of public and private teachers caused a mass exodus of private kindergarten teachers to public schools. Newly qualified graduates from teacher education institutions first seek employment in private schools then, after getting some teaching experience and passing the Licensure Exam for Teachers, they apply to public schools. This means that private schools are training new teachers almost every year.

Implications for other ECEC programmes

Following the New Kindergarten Act, the Department of Social Welfare and Development (DSWD) now supervises childcare programmes, including nursery classes, daycare classes and other pre-kindergarten programmes. Every community has a daycare programme for young children, which includes basic literacy, nutrition and health in its curriculum. Daycare centres in the community also include child protection programmes and projects implemented by the government in co-ordination with local government officials and community leaders.

Nursery classes remain as one of the programmes offered by private schools for children from age three or before entering kindergarten. Nursery classes offer a curriculum that is learner-centred and focuses on the development of young children's social skills and motor skills. Play is the familiar instructional approach for teaching these nursery classes. In both nursery and daycare programmes, there is also a need to employ nurses, dentists, nutritionists and doctors to help teachers meet young children's needs. Daycare teachers receive their salary from either local government or from the national budget through DSWD. Nursery teachers, however, receive their salaries from the private schools. This means their salary is dependent on numbers enrolled and tuition fees collected.

Critical reflections

Early childhood is a very important stage of life. Young children are our most valuable assets or resources. Regardless of race, gender, religion and socio-economic status, they all deserve to be nurtured in a loving, caring and safe environment – the best education and care that every government and private institution can give. Early childhood education and care in the Philippines is far from perfect but Filipinos have tried their best to provide quality education and care to young children – its future leaders and citizens.

Early childhood education and care in the Philippines is neither old nor young considering its historical beginning up to its institutionalisation. Implementation of the New Kindergarten Act provides great opportunities for the government and private sectors to respond to immense challenges clustered around three issues: relevance, quality and access. This means more policies and curricular reforms, professional development for teachers and necessary facilities and instructional support for young children. In particular, with the implementation of kindergarten education in public schools, massive recruitment for qualified kindergarten teachers is needed across the country. This development, however, will not ensure quality and access across the Philippines and there are still many communities without access to ECEC (Pawilen et al, 2006).

Further reading

An update on progress towards global targets for education for all is found in

UNESCO (2000) *DAKAR Framework for Action: Education for All – Meeting Our Collective Commitments.* World Education Forum. Dakar: UNESCO

A country profile of the Philippines was prepared for the Education for All Global Monitoring Report:

UNESCO (2007) *Strong Foundations: Early Childhood Care and Education.* Paris: United Nations Educational, Scientific and Cultural Organization.

This can also be found at unesdoc.unesco.org/images/0014/001472/147225e.pdf (accessed 27 November 2014).

References

Department of Education (2012a) *Standards and Competencies for Five-year-old Filipino Children.* Pasig City: Department of Education.

Department of Education (2012b) *Basic Education Statistics.* Pasig City: Department of Education.

Harris Memorial College (2007) *Student Handbook.*

Lupdag, A D (1999) *The Filipino Preschool Child.* Makati: COGA Publishing.

Magpuri, A M (2002) The Instructional Practices and Their Perceived Effects on the Value Formation in Early Childhood Education. Unpublished thesis. Philippine Normal University, Manila.

National Historical Institute (1993) *Historical Markers: Metropolitan Manila.* Manila: NHI.

Pawilen, G T (2006) *Developing an Indigenous Science Curriculum for Kindergarten in the Philippines.* Unpublished thesis. Ehime University, Japan.

Pawilen, G T (2011) A Model for Developing Curriculum Standards for Pre-service Preschool Teacher Education. Doctoral dissertation. College of Education, University of the Philippines, Diliman, Quezon City.

Pawilen, G T and Sumida, M (2007) Developing an Indigenous Science Curriculum for Kindergarten in the Philippines. *Asia – Pacific Journal of Research in Early Childhood Education,* 1(1): 141–62.

Pawilen, G T, Sumida, M and Fukada, S (2006) A Comparative Analysis of the Kindergarten Curricula of Japan and Philippines, in *Bulletin of the Center for Education and Educational Research of the Faculty of Education,* Ehime University, 24: 27–42.

Pawilen, G T, Sumida, M, Fukada, S and Calingasan, L. (2010) Promoting Cultural Understanding: The Second Phase of Ehime University Student Teaching Experience in the Philippines. Published in *Bulletin of The Center for Educational Research,* Ehime University Faculty of Education, 28: 35–49.

Peralta, J T (2003) *Glimpses: Peoples of the Philippines.* Manila: Anvil Publishing, Inc.

Republic Act 6972 (1991) *An Act Establishing a Day-Care Center in Every Barangay, Instituting Therein a Total Development and Protection of Children Program, Appropriating Funds Thereof and Other Purposes.* Manila: Congress of the Republic of The Philippines.

Republic Act No. 8980 (2000) *An Act Promulgating a Comprehensive Policy and National System for Early Childhood Care and Development, Providing Funds Therefore and Other Purposes.* Manila: Republic of the Philippines.

Republic Act No. 8371 (1997) *The Indigenous Peoples Rights Act of 1997.* Manila: Republic of the Philippine.

Republic Act 10157 (2012) *An Act Institutionalizing the Kindergarten Education into Basic Education System and Appropriating Funds Thereof.* Manila: Republic of the Philippines.

The Republic of the Philippines Constitution (1987). Manila: Congress of the Republic of The Philippines.

UNESCO (2000) *DAKAR Framework for Action: Education for All-Meeting Our Collective Commitments.* World Education Forum. Dakar: UNESCO.

UNESCO (2007) *Strong Foundations: Early Childhood Care and Education.* Paris: UNESCO.

11 Pulling the threads together

JAN GEORGESON AND VERITY CAMPBELL-BARR

Common threads

As we read the chapters in this collection some common themes for Early Childhood Education and Care (ECEC) emerged. Firstly, it is evident that the qualification levels of the ECEC workforce are something that is much debated globally and a number of countries are struggling with the pay and status of ECEC. In addition we see that there are still tensions over what it means to work in ECEC: is it about the care of young children, or their education, or a combination of these two aspects? Many countries are working towards a model of combining care and education in their service delivery, but when different age groups are considered we can see that education is regarded as more applicable for older children, while care is associated with young children. There are also other commonalities that appear throughout the chapters that raise deeper questions about the ECEC workforce.

We would like to share three interconnected threads that became apparent to us as we read through the chapters. We are mindful that other readers might pick up other threads; the following discussion therefore represents one way of synthesising themes from the chapters, and someone else might weave quite a different pattern. The issues we have identified are no doubt well known to educational historians, but there is something rather exciting about finding patterns yourself that makes you want to share what you have found with other people.

The three threads relate to the three sections of the book – pioneers, gender and politics – with Fröbel as the main thread and issues of women in the workforce and global political events intertwining to shape the way Fröbel's ideas were taken up in different contexts (see Figure 11.1) and how women's rights have been perceived.

Fröbel and the kindergarten movement

Fröbel is mentioned in nearly every chapter of the book, frequently at the starting point for development of the early years workforce. Reading Fröbel's works today, this might

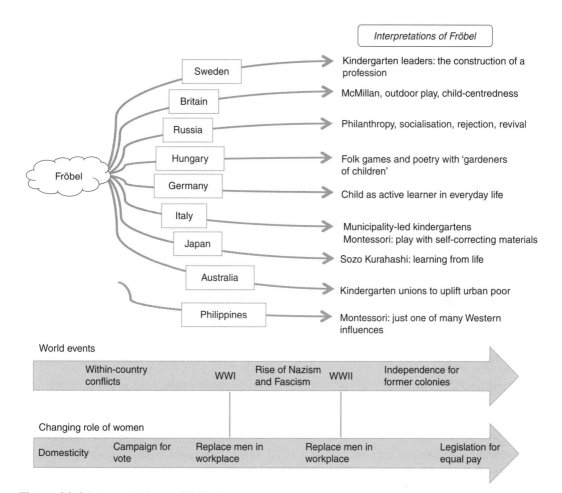

Figure 11.1 *Interpretations of Fröbel*

perhaps seem surprising; many aspects of his writing – the mysticism, the special role of mothers, the complicated coded system of resources and activities – do not sit comfortably with current thinking about training for work with young children. However, at the beginning of the last century, Fröbel's kindergartens represented modernity, a scientific approach to educating young children that resonated with global trends (Wollons, 2000, p 2). It is too simplistic to say kindergartens were an idea whose time had come, but the global diffusion of kindergartens owes much to macro politics and social changes in the role of women. This has been charted in detail and the following discussion draws heavily on ideas put forward in *Kindergartens and Cultures* (Wollons, 2000) and the work of Chung and Walsh (2000).

As we learnt in Chapter 8, Fröbel developed the idea of the kindergarten to realise his vision of appropriate group learning opportunities for all young children, at a time when group care was provided only for children of lower classes, led by male teachers and focused on redeeming children from original sin and subsequent delinquency. Fröbel was steeped in German idealist philosophical traditions, but it is not difficult to trace a direct line from Rousseau's romantic view of children's natural goodness (another common theoretical thread through the chapters), via Pestalozzi's concern for educating the whole child, to Fröbel's vision of early years education that placed the child at the centre. In *The Education of Man*, Fröbel is credited with the first use of *child-centredness*:

> [I]n the period of childhood, [the child] is placed in the centre of all things, and all things are seen only in relation to himself, to his life.
>
> (Fröbel, 1889, p 97)

and it is this concept, together with the importance of developing connections with nature, which more obviously have gone on to underpin early years pedagogy in many countries ever since.

Fröbel's thinking about the optimal conditions for child development prompted him to consider that parents might not manage to provide everything that children needed, and led to the development of kindergartens where children could be together in a safe place with women who had been trained to guide the children through the special activities which Fröbel had developed. Fröbel placed particular importance on the mother figure in children's development, and his ideas seemed to gain more acceptance from women; he therefore began training women as kindergarten teachers and in doing so opened up the profession of teaching to women (Walsh et al, 2001, p 97).

Unfortunately Fröbel's democratic and liberal ideas became associated with nationalism in the period following the failed revolutions of 1848 and in 1851 kindergartens were banned. Fröbel died just a year later and in Germany his ideas have remained perhaps as *potential rather then actual development* (Taylor Allen, in Wollons, 2000, p 16). He would never know the far-ranging influences that his concept of kindergarten would have across the world. In the wake of the ban on kindergartens, Fröbelian scholars fled to Europe and so the kindergarten idea was dispersed first in the West and then across the world.

Sometimes exhibitions publicised kindergarten principles and activities to national and international audiences and awakened interest in the new institution and its associated pedagogy. Those of us who have seen the *Hundred Languages of Children Exhibition* about the pedagogy of Reggio Emilia can attest to the effectiveness of timely exhibitions offering new ideas to people hungry for new ways of doing things. A Fröbel exhibition in London attracted widespread interest; for example Henry Barnard, Secretary of the Connecticut Board of Education, learned about Fröbelian materials and methods at an exhibition in London and then introduced kindergartens to the US in 1854, where the interpretation of these new, modern ideas was played out in the context of the emerging debate about the education of young children and in particular what child-centred means (Chung and Walsh, 2000, p 218). It was this Americanised version of Fröbel's institution which travelled to Australia and to Japan (Wollons, 2000, p 5). In England kindergartens as institutions failed to supplant the public elementary schools despite their appeal to wealthy families (often those slightly outside the mainstream: see Brehony, in Wollons, 2000, p 62) and it was the English infant school which was exported around the world; indeed it is still widely admired, even though English infant schools today have changed greatly in line with 1988 reforms to the education system.

As the idea of kindergarten as a structure travelled round the world, what happened in the kindergartens was shaped by the way in which Fröbel's ideas were assimilated into the local context. Recontextualisation in other contexts meant that specific elements got dropped, or reinterpreted; in Chapter 7 for example we read that in Japan Sozo Kurahashi rejected the formality of Fröbel's gifts and put them all together in a basket for children to explore. In Post-Tsarist Russia, after initial acceptance as a means of socialising children, neo-Froebelianism was denounced as petty-bourgeois pedagogy and disappeared for many years (Valkanova and Brehony, 2006, p 189). The complexity of Fröbel's ideas (and the difficulty for many of understanding what he had written) meant that people had to rely on interpretations of his work and, not surprisingly, these interpretations were shaped by the new context into something which the educators there could understand.

Even though Fröbel's ideas seem benign and do not reflect the communist ideologies that we encountered in Chapter 9 on Hungary, or the fascist ideas in Chapter 4, they nonetheless raise questions about whether complex ideas developed in one country at one time can travel to another. Local cultural interpretation is important, but this can lead to difficulties with subsequent attempts to share understanding. The concept of *child-centred practice* is a case in point; there have been so many reinterpretations of the term that its shared meaning has been diluted.

Critical questions

» *How appropriate is it that one philosophical ideology like Froebelianism has shaped development of the ECEC workforce around the world?*

» *In the chapters in this book, Western philosophies have dominated development of ECEC. Why is this and what might we be missing from failing to acknowledge Eastern approaches to ECEC?*

Women into the workforce

The period when Fröbel's ideas were emerging was a time of social change and social reform. Fröbel's ideas arrived in Russia at a time now widely considered to be an era of great reforms in the country (Valkanova and Brehony, 2006). In England this coincided with the beginnings of the feminist movement and elsewhere powerful women who wanted to make a difference were spearheading educational reforms particularly to help the poorest children in society. Before this time, across Europe opportunities for women to engage in non-manual work outside the home were limited; however, those that did exist included involvement in philanthropic activity (although this was seldom paid work) and the education of young children (as the chapters from Australia and Sweden also demonstrate). Legislative changes had increased the demand for elementary teachers; training opportunities increased but in Britain and elsewhere these were offered mainly by training colleges sponsored by religious organisations, with fewer opportunities for those outside mainstream Christianity.

The deep moral purpose underpinning Fröbel's approach and its focus on young children made work in a kindergarten as suitable occupation for women, while its apparently scientific principles also offered more status than work as a governess or elementary school teacher at that time. As kindergartens spread across Europe, more trained kindergarten teachers were needed who understood Fröbelian principles and the use of the gifts and activities. This was not something that could be picked up on the job; these teachers needed to be trained and, adhering to Fröbelian principles, they needed to be women. Consequently Fröbelian training colleges sprang up first in Europe then around the world, offering women an entry to a profession with a clear moral purpose and recognisable status.

It is also evident as we look across the chapters that ECEC is a feminist issue, both because historically working with children has been constructed as an appropriate activity for women, but also because of ECEC's role over time in supporting women to enter the workforce more widely. What is perhaps troubling about the feminisation of ECEC is the implication that it has for men who want to work with or engage with young children. The number of men working in ECEC remains low across the world and, where parents choose to care for their children at home, the dominant pattern sees mothers undertaking this role.

Critical question

» *We must be careful that the feminist history of the workforce does not exclude men from working in ECEC, and also that fathers do not feel excluded from the care of young children. While there are some clear biological functions that account for the maternal role, what can be done to address the wider assumption that children and their care are regarded as women's issues?*

World wars and civil wars

Internal conflicts in Germany that forced Frobelian scholars out of their own country led to the spread of kindergartens across the world, but the uptake of his ideas was also hastened by the movements in Europe seeking to tame the unruly lower orders and avoid civil war and by the missionary zeal that had accompanied colonial expansion. We could question the extent to which the desire to set up schools for the poor was inspired by philanthropism or by fear of something like the French Revolution happening again if the working classes did not benefit from the civilising influence of education. The effect of both these motivations meant that people were receptive to new ideas about how to educate young children, and Fröbel's adoption of Rousseau's ideals of children's natural goodness must have been attractive.

Looking across the chapters in the book, we also noted how often authors referred to changes in structures for early years provision and increased demands on the workforce in the context of major political events, such as the advent of fascism (Chapter 4) and of Nazism (Chapter 8). In both cases, as in early socialist Russia and in Hungary under communism, early years provision offered the ruling party opportunities to shape children's understanding of society and their place in it, but this made heavy demands on the workforce to carry this through.

The two world wars also changed the progress of women into the workplace in general; World War I showed just how much women could do when they were given the chance, and World War II reinforced this message and in particular showed what women could do when good childcare provision was made available. Peacetime reactions to these global conflicts played out differently in different countries, with different effects on the workforce. In Britain jobs were needed for the men returning from war, so women were encouraged to return to the home and early years provision shrank; in Italy response to fascism led to the establishment of early years provision which would help to ensure that such a regime would not be able to take power again. In Hungary, they found that their national features were excluded from ECEC provision as Soviet systems sought to use kindergarten education as a mechanism for teaching communist ideologies. And in the Philippines, the end of World War II was followed by independence, which was accompanied by a desire to make sure that early years provision met the needs of Filipino children instead of acceptance of whatever successive colonial masters had on offer.

Because of the West's political and economic dominance over the Majority World, Western ideas about what constitutes the right structures, content and pedagogy for ECEC continue to dominate (Holliday, 2010). There is an underlying assumption that Western approaches are superior and this is exacerbated by a longstanding *civilising mission* (Andreotti, 2006, p 41) to bring education to children in far distant lands. Even when a post-colonial stance is adopted and trainers look more carefully at how local cultures are supporting children's development, the deeply entrenched tendency to look to the West can hinder the task of educating new members of the ECEC workforce so that they have the confidence to develop curricula which are respectful of local traditions.

Critical question

» *What is your response to the claim that Western ideas continue to be exported to countries in the Majority World – often with considerable commercial rewards – long after they have achieved independence?*

When we listen to yet another argument about how investment in early years can yield economic benefits for the nation when children grow up and contribute to the workforce, it can sometimes seem as though governments have only just realised how important early years provision is and what a crucial role the early years workforce plays in helping this to happen. Looking at how the workforce has developed on the nine counties in this book reminds us that early years practitioners help to shape children's attitudes too and so contribute to society in much broader and more profound ways.

Critical reflections

When we first had the idea of asking educators from different countries to think about the way that pioneering theorists and political events had shaped the workforce in early education and care, we weren't sure what we'd find. But we were expecting to read a lot about Piaget and Vygotsky – the theorists who have professionalised us. Had we asked our contributors to focus not on the workforce but the curriculum, this might have been the case, but instead, we were surprised to find Fröbel's name cropping up in chapter after chapter, and we realised that we needed to turn round on our own schemata and think more carefully about workforce development in the context – both physical and temporal – in which it was happening, and not through the lens of our own situation in the present day.

Nonetheless we have found echoes of contemporary debates about early years education and care – working with government ideologies that are not one's own, how to cater for the needs of multi-ethnic population – in other countries and in other times and this encourages feelings of solidarity with other early years practitioners who are working through the same problems as us.

We have noted a strong effect of prophets in their own country not having the effect at home which their ideas have abroad. Montessori is more popular outside Italy than in Italy itself; the idea of the English infant school has admirers abroad long after it disappeared under the weight of the demands of the national curriculum and, as we have sketched in this chapter, Fröbel had much more influence outside Germany that he ever did in his own country. This leads one to ponder whether there are great educators in our midst at the moment whom we ignore because they are not as exciting as new ideas from abroad.

Our mapping of Fröbel's influence is just one possible way that ideas have travelled between counties over time. We could have started with Montessori, Malaguzzi or Pestalozzi and produced a different picture. Fröbel was our surprise; the map is our response to that surprise and has prompted us to find out more about him, which has enriched our own understanding of child-centredness – a widely used word that proves curiously difficult to define, or to use with any precision (Stephen, 2010). We invite you to take one idea that surprised you and pursue that by finding your own reading – and then to tell others about it. Talking and reflecting on the ideas that underpin work with young children enriches our understanding of what we do and, rather than deliver curriculum, help us to co-construct an interpretation of curriculum that is appropriate to the children and families with whom we work.

References

Andreotti, V (2006) Soft versus Critical Global Citizenship Education. *Policy and Practice: A Development Education Review*, 3 (Autumn 2006): 40–51.

Chung, S and Walsh, D J (2000) Unpacking Child-Centredness: A History of Meanings. *Journal of Curriculum Studies*, 32(2): 215–34.

Fröbel, F (1889) *The Education of Man.* (W N Hailmann, trans). New York, NY: D Appleton Century. (Original work published in 1826).

Holliday, A (2010) Submission, Emergence, and Personal Knowledge: New Takes and Principles for Validity in Decentred Quality Research, in Shamin, F and Qureshi, R (eds) *Perils, Pitfalls and Reflexivity in Qualitative Research in Education*. Oxford: Oxford University Press.

Stephen, C (2010) Pedagogy: The Silent Partner in Early Years Learning. *Early Years*, 30(3): 15–28.

Valkanova, Y and Brehony, K J (2006) The Gifts and 'Contributions': Friedrich Froebel and Russian Education (1850–1929). *History of Education*, 35(2): 189–207.

Walsh, D J, Chung, S and Tufekci, A (2001) Friedrich Wilhelm Froebel, 1782–1852, in Palmer, J A (ed) *Fifty Major Thinkers on Education From Confucius to Dewey*. Milton Park: Routledge, pp 94–9.

Wollons, R (2000) *Kindergartens and Cultures: The Global Diffusion of an Idea*. New Haven: Yale University Press.

Index

Notes and Reflections